LEADING WITH

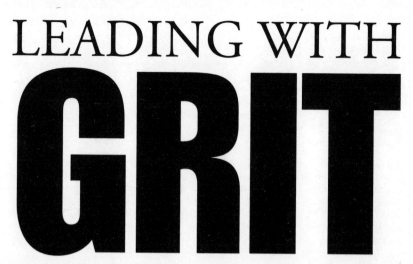

GRIT

Inspiring Action and Accountability with
Generosity, Respect, Integrity, and Truth

LAURIE SUDBRINK

Cover image: Jade Whaley
Cover design: Jade Whaley
Photo credit: Jeff Palm

This book is printed on acid-free paper.

GRIT is a registered trademark.

Published by John Wiley & Sons, Inc., Hoboken, New Jersey
Published simultaneously in Canada

Limit of Liability/Disclaimer of Warranty: While the publisher and author have used their best efforts in preparing this book, they make no representations or warranties with the respect to the accuracy or completeness of the contents of this book and specifically disclaim any implied warranties of merchantability or fitness for a particular purpose. No warranty may be created or extended by sales representatives or written sales materials. The advice and strategies contained herein may not be suitable for your situation. You should consult with a professional where appropriate. Neither the publisher nor the author shall be liable for damages arising herefrom.

For general information about our other products and services, please contact our Customer Care Department within the United States at (800) 762-2974, outside the United States at (317) 572-3993 or fax (317) 572-4002.

Wiley publishes in a variety of print and electronic formats and by print-on-demand. Some material included with standard print versions of this book may not be included in e-books or in print-on-demand. If this book refers to media such as a CD or DVD that is not included in the version you purchased, you may download this material at http://booksupport.wiley.com. For more information about Wiley products, visit www.wiley.com.

Library of Congress Cataloging-in-Publication Data is Available
ISBN 978-1-118-97522-0 (Hardback)
ISBN 978-1-118-97563-3 (ePDF)
ISBN 978-1-118-97562-6 (ePub)

Printed in the United States of America

10 9 8 7 6 5 4 3 2 1

This book is dedicated to my late brother, Thomas Dalton Sudbrink.
Coincidentally Tommy was a cowboy who taught me a lot about GRIT®

CONTENTS

PART III   Your Impact

 **PREFACE**

We all have our challenges in life. Some of those challenges we make for ourselves, while some are what we inherit. Looking back, I realize that in my early years I was too focused on what I didn't have and what I thought I should have had. As I became more aware of myself and my surroundings, I could see that it's not so much about what you have; it's more important what you do with it. Life is a little like poker—we don't pick the cards; we can only do our best with the hand we're dealt. And be grateful that we even get to play the game!

Throughout college and in my first few jobs, I noticed a negativity that many of us seemed to have about going to school and work. People, including myself, acted as if they were trapped and had no choice. It was crazy how miserable we made ourselves with our own thoughts and beliefs! I could remember that when I was very young, I was positive and happy, always looking for the best in other people. But somewhere along the way, I became cynical and sarcastic, because it seemed like that's what you had to do to connect with others, and survive emotionally. Pretty soon this became the norm and it felt familiar and comfortable.

It was a college professor who first opened my mind to the power of my thoughts and beliefs. I was taking evening classes as

I worked full time. Being a single mom, Dr. Thomas Mwanika in the Communications Department allowed me to bring my 7-year-old daughter to class with me from time to time. It was probably a combination of Dr. Mwanika's influence, the course material in general semantics, and my daughter's interest and grasp of the meaning of words and their influence that began my journey back to me. Ever since, I've been on a continuous path of self-awareness and conscious living. One of the many important lessons I continue to embrace is to be aware, without judgment, and do my best. The more I give up the need to be perfect, the better life gets.

Unlike most leadership books, this book begins by focusing on you as an individual. It is intended to accelerate your awareness, and is the foundation to great leadership. It provides a foundation that will help you take responsibility for your life, and enjoy your journey. It helps you answer questions about what is important to you and guides you through making better choices. After working with thousands of people from a variety of industries over the past 15 years, coupled with over a decade of experience as an employee, it became obvious to me that we need to start inside, with our own thoughts and beliefs. Only when we make a shift there will we authentically change our actions and behaviors. When we are happy and whole, we will then be able to intentionally lead others.

Leadership is not a position—it is a calling. Whether we're in a formal position in an organization, contributing our technical expertise, home raising children, or people just naturally turn to you for advice—each of us has an opportunity to make a difference. The question is, what difference do you want to make?

I knew writing this book would be a lot of work when I first outlined the chapters on a flight from New York to San Diego about 10 years ago. I was inspired and committed to sharing this message, and I'm forever grateful for the experience. As with any great challenge, I've learned so much more about myself and my work.

I believe we are all messengers; it's not that we're creating it all from scratch—it's more about the way we share it with others. Generosity, respect, integrity, and truth are words we are all familiar with. In the unique combination of GRIT®, a path is paved for happiness, success, and leadership. I'm grateful and honored that you are reading my book, and I hope you will use it to inspire action and accountability for you and the people you influence.

Cheers!

WITH GRATITUDE

Feeling gratitude and not expressing it is like wrapping a present and not giving it.

—William Arthur Ward

First and foremost I'd like to thank my mom, Margaret Davis, not only for helping with input on the book, but for her unconditional love, support, and encouragement. She is the strongest, most brilliant and compassionate woman I know.

Next I am deeply and forever grateful to my daughter, Jade Whaley, who has been by my side through the entire book, from the very beginning when it was just a concept thought up on a five-hour plane trip. Jade has supported, encouraged, poked holes, and challenged—giving me exactly what I needed. Not only is she a fantastic daughter, she's extremely talented and objective as well. I couldn't be more blessed.

My heartfelt appreciation also goes out to two people who were with me in the early stages of the book and were invaluable in helping me develop my book proposal and sample chapters—Ray Justice and Jennifer Loew; and to Gina Mangiemeli, who helped me with the start-up of my business and has been a friend and supporter ever since. Thank you for your continued support and belief in me; you are my very dear friends.

Many thanks go out to Roseanne Romero and my team at Unlimited Coaching Solutions in the early days for helping me come up with the GRIT® acronym. And special thanks to Roseanne, who has been a good friend and has provided input on GRIT® throughout the years.

I am so grateful for the help from Vickie Curry and her husband Steve. From tirelessly reading chapters and providing feedback, to supporting and encouraging me and hosting me at their home. Thank you, Vickie—you are always encouraging and positive, yet direct and helpful.

Thank you so much to my talented, generous, and very positive nieces, Taylor Ellis for research and Kari Whaley for edits; to my friend Kristine Predmore for assistance with chapter review; and to my sister-in-law Marcy Sudbrink for general support as well. I am thankful for the editing help of Lara Lui, Lisa Fugard, and Lois Weston-Bernstien at different stages of the book.

Early in my life, there were a few people who influenced me, and, without them, I may not be where I am today. Thank you Mr. Keith Aggott, Mrs. Eleanor Harvey, Dr. Thomas Mwanika, Dr. Tony Papalia, John Pointkowski, and Don Miguel Ruiz. You made a difference in my life.

To all my family, friends, LinkedIn, and Facebook supporters: Thank you so much for sticking with me, providing comments and answering questions, and just being there. You inspired me—and continue to do so.

And a very special thanks to my clients who provided me with the opportunity for many of the stories and examples herein. Of course I've kept you confidential; I am forever grateful for everything you've shared with me.

Thank you to my friend Todd MacDonald, who has provided unwavering support throughout. And a special acknowledgement to my faithful companion Mason who helped me stay balanced and happy-forever in my heart.

And thank you Peter Wiley, Lisa Shannon, and Matt Davis for giving me this opportunity.

I am blessed with so much inspiration and so many lessons from numerous people throughout my life that have contributed to this book. Thank you to all of you who have touched my life.

● INTRODUCTION

Ask yourself what is really important, and then have the wisdom and courage to build your life around your answer.

—Lee Jampolsky

We've all worked at places we dreaded going to every day: jobs where we didn't feel valued, trusted, or heard; places devoid of trust, effective communication, and true motivation. In workplaces like these, loyalty goes out the window, little work gets done, and everyone looks out for themselves. Meanwhile, as we suffer, so does the quality of the product or service we're providing. Ultimately, no one is happy. We feel taken advantage of, overwhelmed, and helpless to make changes, and our employer is frustrated by the lack of productivity of his employees. When experiencing these feelings, most of us will gossip rather than communicate openly, blame others rather than examine our own behavior, make assumptions rather than ask for clarification. These behaviors are at the root of a toxic workplace. We may get instant gratification from belittling our coworkers or supervisors, but such behavior doesn't solve the problem and may actually create new ones. Workplaces like these are full of people who feel miserable, stuck, and unappreciated.

This particular form of unhappiness—workplace misery— generates big business. Movies have been made about it; hundreds of books offer counsel on it. Thousands, if not millions, of people have been told to picture their bosses while throwing punches in kickboxing class, and the initials T.G.I.F. have spawned a chain of restaurants. In all my years of working with organizations I can certainly attest to the presence of workplace misery.

Your workplace may not be a total disaster, but it could probably be improved. Perhaps it could benefit from a decrease in the complaining, or more willingness to share information, or maybe just a little less stress and a little more productivity. Whatever the level of misery, there is usually room for improvement. Sometimes a one- to two-degree shift in perspective can produce a big difference. And if we are mindful of some simple concepts, we can make that shift.

Leading with GRIT® provides a road map to improve individual and organizational health. In today's challenging times, we need tough characters to get the job done. While grit—having courage, resolution and fortitude—is something we strive for in our personal and professional lives, GRIT® provides the way.

The first step is becoming aware that effecting change is a choice. Then, with a desire to make a change, the next step is to learn the principles of GRIT®—generosity, respect, integrity, and truth. It is not only the concepts of GRIT®, but how they are combined, that make them so effective. Applying GRIT® creates personal accountability, inspires ourselves and others to do their best, enhances team performance, and develops authentic leadership. The outcome is a more fulfilling, satisfying, and, yes, profitable, experience for individuals and the organizations they work for. In a workplace with GRIT®, it's possible to enjoy work more, feel less stress, and be more creative, productive, trusting, and open. Managers will come to fully appreciate that a paycheck cannot be their employees' sole motivation for their work. It's simple with GRIT® to appreciate others for doing things right and rec‑ognize them for it while simultaneously helping them be more accountable. And employees will better understand their respon‑sibility in achieving a more enjoyable workplace. The payoff is employee retention, increased innovation and productivity, and a more positive and profitable workplace.

Understanding and adhering to the principles of GRIT® takes determination and perseverance. Not because the elements in GRIT® are difficult, but because we are creatures of habit. Most people are not consciously choosing their thoughts, beliefs, and behaviors. Therefore, GRIT® is for people who want to get results and are willing to do the work that it takes to change habits and get those results. With practice, written guidelines, and practical advice, leading with GRIT® can become a reality for anyone who wants to minimize workplace misery.

The intent of this book is to help people navigate through the tough times and free themselves from the chokehold of negativity. Using the methods that are shared within these pages, thousands have learned to embrace GRIT® worldwide. While it is meant to be a practical leadership guide for transforming the workplace, it can also serve as an individual's path to personal freedom.

Leading with GRIT® is organized into 12 chapters, with three parts. Part I is geared toward the individual, and is foundational to your success as a leader. It explains choice and each of the GRIT® elements—generosity, respect, integrity, and truth. The Five Steps of Change™ is included to help guide you through the changes you choose to make. This first part is a crucial foundation for the kind of leadership we need today. Part II focuses on communicating with GRIT®—making communication easier, more enjoyable and more productive. It is relevant to any area of your life, and it is particularly important for your role as a leader. Part III is how, in our role as leaders, we apply and sustain GRIT® in the workplace, creating systems that help keep everyone on track. The stories and examples are all real. Names of organizations and individuals have been changed in respect for my clients' privacy.

At the end of each chapter, a step-by-step guide is provided to help you reflect on what you've read, and what you'd like to focus your attention on so you can make a SHIFT:

Scan the chapter. List the topics that resonated with you.

Hone in on one or two areas that will make the biggest impact for you.

Imagine the impact. Why is this important? How will you feel when you've accomplished this?

Figure out your plan and how you will stay on track.

Take action. Start now. Schedule it now and include your follow-up.

Enjoy! Remember to choose to be happy, every step of the way!

Although everyone navigates books differently, for this book I suggest that you read it through first to fully understand the concepts and the uniqueness of how they are combined. While they are linear to some degree, the GRIT® concepts are also very intertwined. At the end of Chapter 1, there is an assessment to help provide a framework and a personal awareness of GRIT®. The personal work in Part I is crucial before moving on. Some people may prefer to read Part I all the way through, then come back to each chapter in Part I before moving to Parts II and III.

While doing the SHIFT exercises at the end of each chapter, go back to the individual concepts you found most challenging. Each GRIT® concept can be used as an awareness tool as well. If you find you're out of integrity, it's a great opportunity to look back at your truth. If you're not feeling generous or you're overdoing it, look back at respect, integrity, and/or truth. Keep the book handy as a reference and reminder. Proactively review concepts. And whenever you're feeling stuck, overwhelmed, or frustrated, turn to *Leading with GRIT*® for some help.

Leading with GRIT® moves beyond the theoretical frameworks commonly taught in business school and emphasizes value-based principles and personal development in a pragmatic approach. *Leading with GRIT*® is for both employees and employers—whether you are an entrepreneur or manager, in a formal or informal leadership role, this book is meant to be your guide—to inspire you, to motivate you, and to lead you to make a difference for yourself and others. Enjoy your journey.

CHAPTER ONE

FREEDOM TO CHOOSE

Stop chasing happiness and start choosing happiness.

—Unknown

Remember the last vacation you took and how you felt while you were getting ready to go? It was exciting! You were passionate and energized just by the thought of it. While you imagined the white sand beaches, the sun warming your skin, and the sound of the waves crashing, your workdays leading up to your departure went by faster, you worked harder, and you were happier.

Now let me ask if you ever felt this way about going to work. Most people answer no to this question. In fact, they look at me as if to say, "Are you nuts? Why would I feel this way about going to work?"

I remember feeling this negative about work myself, years ago when I worked for a manufacturing company in upstate New York. On a typical rainy, windy spring day, after dropping papers into a puddle and having my umbrella flip inside out, I trudged into the lobby, trying to sneak past our overly cheerful receptionist. But she caught me with her usual chipper greeting, "Good morning, Laurie! How are you this morning?" "I'm having a bad day," I muttered begrudgingly. In a dramatic gesture, she whipped her arm almost out of its socket to show her watch and exclaimed, "Wow, and it's only 7 A.M.!" At this point, I wanted to leap across the counter and choke her. It hit me as I walked away that I was *choosing* to let this bother me. How I was acting and reacting was a choice. All of a sudden it was clear to me that I was making myself miserable. It was as if a fog had been wiped away from the mirror and I could see. I had a choice. I could choose to be positive or negative. Rather than letting my mind control me, I could focus my thoughts and attention where I wanted them to be. As the fog continued to clear, I began to realize the amount of freedom and self-control I was gaining!

The Choice is Yours

I am who I am today because of the choices I made yesterday.

—Eleanor Roosevelt

Many of our experiences are based on the choices we make, either consciously or subconsciously. Our life is a reflection of our own beliefs and choices, and often we don't even realize that we are making choices. Sadly, it usually takes tragedies, near-death experiences, getting fired, or other forms of loss to wake us up. When these life events happen, reality hits us so hard that it makes us aware of life and the choices we have. But do we really need that kind of shock treatment to wake us up? Experiencing a tragedy is also no guarantee that we will wake up and recognize our options and choices. Just imagine if we could become aware and see the value of making positive changes in our lives without first enduring that tragedy. We could realize our plight and potentially prevent negative repercussions, all by making different choices.

We can't always control what happens in life, but we can control the way we react to it. We can blame others or bad luck, or we can ask ourselves what we can learn from our experiences. We can use the faith we have in ourselves and other people to help us through. We can choose to live life to the fullest and do our best with the hand we're dealt. We can find humor in the situation and lighten up a little. Just making a choice to be grateful, appreciative, and happy will return joy to our lives, at work and at home.

I was reminded of this recently when my friend Mike was telling me about his first week at his new job. He previously worked in a physical job, as a mechanic, but switched careers to road construction. Mike's plan was to move up the ladder and become supervisor, but he wanted to start where everyone else did, on the road, laying pavement. Mike admitted that after the first couple of days on the job, he was pretty sore and honestly thinking, "Wow, this is really hard stuff!" He noticed an older man, who looked to be in his 60s, plugging away like the Energizer Bunny in the battery commercials. Mike eventually worked his way over to strike up a conversation with the man because he was curious as to how this guy did it. He complimented him in that tough construction guy sort of way: "Hey man, you've got to be pushing 60 or so, how do you have so much energy? I mean, really, why are you still here, still working?" The man's reply was shocking. He said, "Actually, I'm 82, and I can't wait to come to work every day. I love it. It keeps me young and alive!"

As Mike and his new coworker talked more and more, Mike discovered that this guy had figured out what he wanted from life, and he had built his life around that. He was genuinely positive and did not dwell on all the negatives. He chose to be happy, and you could see the payoff in his health, his attitude, and his productivity.

Of course, we're not all naturally like this. And the construction worker may not have always been that way, either. In fact, in my experience, a lot of people at some point in their lives need help with choosing a positive attitude. And being positive at work can sometimes be very challenging. A lot of people suffer through each day, counting down the minutes, waiting and wishing their weekdays away for the weekend, for vacation, for anything other than the time they are spending at work. Considering how much time you spend at work, you're spending a lot of time choosing to be negative.

What if we were able to think about it differently? What if we could make some different choices? Perhaps we could become as positive as the 82-year-old Energizer Bunny. Since my 7 A.M. wake-up call on that rainy day in upstate New York, I have been on a path to continuously improve my own awareness and growth and to focus on being more positive. It has definitely entailed making different choices.

The definition of insanity is doing the same thing over and over and expecting a different result. Yet isn't that what we continually do? We repeat the same behavior and then complain when things aren't different. So if we took a different approach at work, shouldn't we be guaranteed to produce a different result?

I'm not suggesting a radical change. I'm talking about going back to some basics, tried-and-true principles that have been proven effective. Since change is inevitable, maybe we can play a role in how change unfolds, rather than just let it happen. It's like a farmer and his crops. He can plant seeds, leave them alone, and hope for the best, or he can weed, prune, and water his plants, and the farm will yield a robust crop.

There's no doubt we need a change, not only for our own health and happiness but also because today's organizations will have a difficult time surviving the current competitive marketplace, with its ever-changing technology and the pressure to do more with less. We need leaders who are intentional in developing the culture and the individuals therein. Being an intentional leader begins with knowing ourselves and staying true to ourselves. Then we can give authentically to others. Practicing GRIT®—generosity, respect, integrity, and truth—will enable us to focus on the right issues, develop ourselves and our teams, and create more with less. We might not have much control over the direction of the marketplace, but we can make a big impact with the way we lead.

Once we become aware that we have a choice, we can begin to examine and change our beliefs, beginning with believing that we can make a positive impact. When we choose to cultivate the right mind-set with GRIT®, it is possible. Being able to visualize what it could be like and how it would feel propels us into action. However, without an open mind and a positive attitude, there will be no foundation to build upon.

Take a moment to visualize how it would feel if you couldn't wait to get to work. Think about it from the moment you wake up. What would your thoughts and feelings be? How would it affect what you did in the morning, how you interacted with your family, what you wore, how much time you gave yourself to get ready? Do you think you'd feel rushed and stressed, or relaxed and happy? And imagine that when you reach your workplace in the morning, you're greeted by coworkers who are genuinely happy to be there. They take the time to smile and say hello, and they really are interested when they say, "How are you today?" Everyone communicates openly and to the point, without holding back for fear of upsetting someone or rocking the boat. There are no triangulated conversations (full of he said, she said). And when people receive direct communication, they don't get defensive. They listen objectively, consider what is being said, and reply openly, immediately. They do not feel frustrated, angry, or defensive in any way. Everyone's goal is to understand each other, be as productive as possible, and have a good time. Even when they disagree, there is open communication: "I'm just not seeing it that way; can we talk about it a little more?" and the receiver of that message simply says, "Sure, when's a good time?" They continue to go about their business, without wasting time brooding over a misunderstanding. People are generally happy, productive, and completely engaged.

Sound impossible? Consider this: Would you agree that your thoughts about going on vacation are what get you energized and motivated, not necessarily the event itself? You haven't actually felt the warm sun on your skin or heard the sound of waves crashing on the beach, but just thinking about being there puts you in a good mood.

On the other hand, have you ever been excited about attending a New Year's Eve event, only to be disappointed when it didn't live up to your expectations? You had high hopes for the evening, only to be disappointed when it wasn't as fabulous as you imagined.

Think about how much your thoughts control your emotions and feelings. If our thoughts create the mood we're in, could we not change our thoughts about work? Some of you might be thinking, "Work is not at all like a vacation or a fun event, so how could I have positive thoughts about work? Won't I be setting myself up for disappointment, like the New Year's Eve example?" The reality is that just like anticipating New Year's Eve, we're not able to control what actually happens. But we can choose our attitude, how we react, and where to focus our attention.

Consider the aspects you do like about work. Maybe there are only one or two things. Perhaps what you do is having a positive impact on children, or maybe you enjoy helping certain teammates or customers. It could be as simple as appreciating that your upcoming vacation is made possible by this job, or it could be the overall flexibility you enjoy. What is your bigger purpose related to your job? You may not be in your dream job or have found your passion yet, but focusing on the positive aspects will help you get clear on your intentions for being in this position. Whether you love what you do or you're doing it to be able to do what you love, either way, you can choose to put your whole self into it. When you're clear on why you're in this job, you can accept that you chose this job, for whatever reason or motivation, and you can choose to be positive and enjoy it while you're here.

Now you may be thinking, "Okay, I've found *my* motivation and I'm being positive, but I can't control all the other negativity around me." Be honest with yourself and consider what, if anything, you might be doing to create, support, or enable the workplace negativity. Do you believe you have any role in it at all? Or is it someone else's fault, like your boss, the team you're on, the owner, or even the board?

This isn't to say that it's always you who needs to change. But if you are doing everything you can to be positive and productive, then it's much clearer when it really is the environment that's negative, not you. Sure, it can be frustrating when you're in a negative environment—you can maintain your positive attitude for only so long. But you'll be able to quickly discern this and make a change for yourself, rather than suffering through it, feeling helpless.

Following a formula for creating your own happiness at work simultaneously creates a healthier company. It's a win–win for both employee and employer. The company can then make a bigger difference in its community, in its country, and, hey, maybe even a little difference in the world. The method is tried-and-true and was used by countless companies worldwide even before it got its name.

When combined and applied, the four elements of GRIT® (see Figure 1.1) free us to create a healthier, happier, and more productive experience for ourselves and for our workplace.

GRIT® is a mind-set that ensures you're doing your best. Through GRIT®, we learn how to take a look at ourselves on a deeper level. We see that how we're treating ourselves, what we're doing and saying to ourselves, directly influences the way we are treating other people. GRIT® exercises our mental equipment to ensure that it's in the best possible shape to properly overcome any challenge.

It's similar to making sure your car is in tip-top shape so you'll have the best adventure you can have. Your gas tank is full,

Figure 1.1. The Four Elements of GRIT®

your oil has been changed, and your tires are the right pressure. You're in alignment—you're fine-tuned and ready for anything! It's widely accepted that we need to spend time improving our physical being and even, to some degree, our intellect—but what about our mental and emotional being? If we leave just one element out, like not changing the oil, the car will eventually break down.

Many studies have linked illness to our mental state. In 2003, Gallup linked misery at work with unhappiness at home. In March 2010, *Science Daily* (2010) reported that chronic job stress and lack of physical activity are strongly associated with being overweight or obese. Elizabeth Heubeck of WebMD (2007) wrote that a toxic work atmosphere can lead to deteriorating health. Results from a GAZEL study (2012) indicate that "poor psychosocial working conditions are prospectively linked to reduced health functioning, in particular mental health functioning." Showing a link to stress and our health is not saying that it's the only cause of any illness; if someone has cancer, it doesn't mean it was definitely caused by stress. But it has been proven that stress can be at least a factor in causing or worsening illnesses. I've witnessed this firsthand in numerous clients over the years, and I'm sure most of you have had some experience with stress and illness.

Not only does our mental and emotional state impact our health but also it affects the way we participate in any relationship, professional or personal. It's difficult to successfully function in any relationship without knowing ourselves and having integrity by making the right choices to support what we want and need. Only then can we authentically give to any relationship.

With all the data and information we have, the question arises, why wouldn't people take care of their thoughts and better manage their thoughts? Perhaps it's too intangible to measure. Or they don't believe it's possible. Or they aren't yet aware that they can control their own stress. Or they don't have a way to do it.

It all starts with your relationship with yourself. GRIT® is the tool to fine-tune your mental equipment. So what do you think? Are you ready to explore GRIT®?

Before moving into the next four chapters on GRIT®, I recommend taking some time to reflect on the brief GRIT® assessment provided on the following pages (see Figure 1.2). We'll get more in-depth on the key areas in the coming chapters. This assessment is designed as a framework for understanding the GRIT® concepts and as a self-awareness tool.

Although there is scoring, it is meant for your personal development. Be as objective and honest as possible with yourself while answering. It's not a test. The GRIT® assessment will help you become more aware of yourself and where you are coming from. This will give you a starting point as we work through the book.

You can approach the interpretation of the assessment in two ways. After you've circled the number that best suits you for each phrase, you can just reflect on the statements and have a basic

TRUTH						
I control my thoughts.	5	4	3	2	1	My thoughts control me.
I know my natural strengths and challenges and I accept myself.	5	4	3	2	1	I'd rather not know what my strengths and challenges are.
I trust my intuition; I use it in decision making.	5	4	3	2	1	I would never rely on intuition; you have to have all the details and facts to decide.
I take time to be still and reflect; I consider myself very aware.	5	4	3	2	1	I don't have time to sit still; my mind is always busy.
I believe I'm supposed to be happy; it is my choice. I focus on the positive.	5	4	3	2	1	I don't believe happiness is a choice; some people are luckier than others.
I am clear on what's important to me to feel successful and authentic.	5	4	3	2	1	I don't really know what I want.
I know my values and priorities in life.	5	4	3	2	1	I justify "other" values when it's convenient; I'm not really sure what I believe in.
My past doesn't predict my future; I am who I choose to be.	5	4	3	2	1	There's not much I can do to change; I am who I am.
Truth Total:						

INTEGRITY						
I do what I say I'm going to do.	5	4	3	2	1	I often change appointments and have to cancel things.
I can confidently say no, without guilt.	5	4	3	2	1	I say yes to please others, even at my own expense; I don't feel like I can say no.
I am aware that my actions influence others.	5	4	3	2	1	My actions and words shouldn't affect others; people are responsible for themselves.
I take on what I can handle; I know my limits.	5	4	3	2	1	I take on more than I should but if I don't I won't advance in my career.
I don't hide truths from myself or people who are important to me.	5	4	3	2	1	I stretch the truth to impress, or I hide truths from people.
I have lots of energy and feel purposeful at work, and afterwards.	5	4	3	2	1	I feel stretched and overwhelmed at work; I dread Mondays.
I don't hold back saying what is important to say.	5	4	3	2	1	I refrain from saying a lot of things I probably should say; or I say way too much.
I keep focused on what's important and align my activities appropriately.	5	4	3	2	1	I'm so busy I feel like I can just barely handle what's coming at me.
Integrity Total:						

RESPECT						
I value my time and others' time equally.	5	4	3	2	1	It's hard enough to get my own stuff done; I can't think of other people's time.
I realize everyone has their own truth, and I don't know their whole story.	5	4	3	2	1	It's obvious what other people are thinking and feeling.
I adapt to effectively communicate with others.	5	4	3	2	1	I communicate consistently in my own style; people can take it or leave it.
I feel confident 'sitting at the table' with other successful people.	5	4	3	2	1	I feel 'not as good as' or 'better than' others.
I allow other people to have their own experiences; I respect their choices and opinions.	5	4	3	2	1	I jump in to help other people make decisions, and give my opinion and advice.
I can understand and empathize with different perceptions.	5	4	3	2	1	Most things are black and white; true or false.
I delegate all appropriate tasks and I feel good about it.	5	4	3	2	1	I can't delegate tasks because there's no one available or qualified.
I realize the things people do are not 'all about me.'	5	4	3	2	1	I feel people rarely consider me and my feelings.
Respect Total:						

GENEROSITY						
I have enough time to do the most important things.	5	4	3	2	1	I don't have enough time to get things done.
I feel good about where I am in my career, my relationship(s), my life.	5	4	3	2	1	I wish I were somewhere else, someone else, doing something else.
I am willing to set my tasks aside to help others, but not at the expense of myself.	5	4	3	2	1	I frequently jump in and help others and then resent it because I didn't get my own work done.
I am happy for others' success – there's enough to go around for everyone.	5	4	3	2	1	I feel jealous of others' success. I fear if they are successful then I can't be.
I feel good about being happy.	5	4	3	2	1	I feel guilty about being happy.
I look forward to going home at night and I have the energy for personal priorities.	5	4	3	2	1	I have no energy left at the end of the day for my personal interests or priorities.
I feel grateful for what I have; I'm content and satisfied.	5	4	3	2	1	I constantly want more; I often wish I had what I don't have.
I mindfully stay present and listen fully.	5	4	3	2	1	I check out while listening because I have a lot going on in my own world.
Generosity Total:						

Grand Total:		

Figure 1.2. GRIT® Self Assessment

awareness of your score. Or you can tally up your total score and read the suggestions for each total. Either way, you can use the assessment throughout your progress and keep rechecking yourself to hone in on areas you wish to improve. As you take the assessment, and as you venture through each chapter, remember to enjoy your journey.

GRIT® Self-Awareness Assessment

- In selecting the number that is closest to your true statement, on the left or on the right, remember to be objective and honest with yourself. This is for your eyes only. It is not a test.
- When you find yourself saying, "It depends," do your best to select the appropriate number for your most likely scenarios.

Because the purpose of this assessment is to provide a framework for GRIT® and for your own self-awareness, it's up to you how you'd like to interpret it. Here are a couple of suggestions:

- Simply scan your answers and be mindful of them as you read through the upcoming chapters.

- If you prefer to obtain a score, add each section and then add all four sections.

Each section pertains to a GRIT® concept, and you'll be able to see your highest and lowest scores. The lowest score per section is 8, and the highest is 40.

The lowest total assessment score is 32, and the highest total score is 160. Remember, this isn't a test: if you get the lowest score that doesn't mean you failed. Recognizing and accepting where you are, without judgment, is the first step toward self-improvement.

Total Score Suggestions

32–70   As you probably realized while taking the assessment, your GRIT® may be a bit out of alignment, and that's okay. In fact, it's great because you now have the tool you need to increase your GRIT®—this book! Congratulations for taking the first step. As you are reading through the upcoming chapters, continue to practice being aware without judging yourself. As you notice an emotion or a resistance, just notice it. Accept it. Practice being as open as possible, while also questioning things. If you find that difficult, reread Chapter 1 and skip to Chapter 6. Then go back to Chapters 2 through 5.

71–121 You may have noticed that some areas were higher for you and some were lower. Since you're right in the middle of the road, pick a few areas that you feel would benefit you the most, and begin by focusing on those areas. As you read through the upcoming chapters, continue to be aware of those areas, and notice if there's any resistance. Continue to question while balancing that healthy skepticism with being open to consider other ways. As you increase your GRIT® in the focus areas that you initially chose, you can retake the assessment to see your improvement and then refocus on other areas to continue your development.

122–160 If you scored in this category, then you're most likely already living with GRIT®, and most likely leading that way, too. Because you scored here, you probably agree that there's always room for improvement. As you reflect over your assessment, be aware of any areas in which you scored lower than a 3, and as you read the upcoming chapters, continue to reflect on these areas, especially as you consider your leadership role.

No matter what your score, the goal here is to provide a framework and an awareness that leads to development of your leadership skills. Don't be too hard on yourself. Enjoy the journey and have fun as you work your way through this book.

Each of Chapters 2 through 12 contains a reflection called SHIFT at the end. As you are completing this reflection exercise, take a moment to come back to this assessment. Feel free to adjust any of your selections if you feel differently. Reviewing the assessment may help you hone in on an area of focus for you.

And remember, make it a conscious choice to enjoy your journey!

References

Gallup (2003). Bringing Work Problems Home. Washington, DC: Crabtree, S. Huebeck, E. (2007). Workplace Stress and Your Health. WebMD. Retrieved from http://www.webmd.com/men/features/work-stress.

University of Rochester Medical Center. (2010). Study Connects Workplace
    Turmoil, Stress and Obesity. *Science Daily*. Retrieved from
    www.sciencedaily.com/releases/2010/03/100324142133.htm.
Wahrendorf, M., Sembajwe, G., Zins, M., Berkman, L., Goldberg, M.,
    Siegrist, J. (2012). Long-term Effects of Psychosocial Work Stress in
    Midlife on Health Functioning After Labor Market Exit—Results From
    the GAZEL Study. *The Journals of Gerontology Series B: Psychologi-
    cal Sciences and Social Sciences*, 67(4), 471–480. doi:10.1093/geronb/
    gbs045.

PART I

GRIT®—THE FOUNDATION

GRIT® is the foundation we need to lead effectively. Part I focuses on our individual development of GRIT®.

Part II will focuse on communicating with GRIT®—making communication easier, more enjoyable, and more productive. Part III will hone in on implementing GRIT® as a leader in the workplace.

CHAPTER TWO

TRUTH—THE CORE

Wanting to be someone else is a waste of the person you are.

—Kurt Cobain

I never realized how lost I was—how many masks I wore, just trying to please others around me. Did this come from being a middle child in a large family? Was it the guilt trips put on me as a child that made me too worried about what others thought about me? Or was it just something I was born with? I'm not entirely sure, but what I do know is that it negatively affected my life—at work and personally. At times, I would take on so much, and then feel like a victim for being taken advantage of. It seemed to me that the situation was totally out of my control, and I felt no responsibility for getting myself there. The more work I would agree to do, the more positive attention I seemed to be getting. Even my family and friends were feeling sorry for me for "the way corporate treated me." Little did I know it was depleting me

and I was on the verge of burnout. Yes, somewhere I
had taken a turn and was becoming disengaged.
I didn't want to come to work. When I was there,
I couldn't really concentrate—I may have been at
50 percent capacity at times. This went on for
years.... until I discovered my truth.

We've all heard the expression the truth will set you free. It
dates back to biblical times when Jesus said, "you will know
the truth, and the truth will set you free" (John 8:32 ESV). Only
once you discover your truth—what's important for you—will you
be free to live the life you want. You'll be able to make choices that
are based on your truth, giving you the freedom to be truly happy.

Discovering your truth is significant because everything
stems from it, affecting us both personally and professionally—
especially in the way we lead others. Taking time to self-reflect
and getting to know our core self produces gratifying results,
at work and elsewhere.

Truth is a very deep topic, and the word itself has many different connotations. For the purposes of GRIT®, we are defining
personal truth, and this includes a few components. It begins with
a more global belief in your own potential and your purpose here
to be happy. It is what is important to you—your purpose, your
intent, your *why*. It is who you are and what you believe in. Truth
is comprised of your passions and priorities, your strengths and
your challenges, and knowing your goals and where you want to
be. It is also about your reality in this moment in time, your tendencies, your preferences, and your thoughts and beliefs. It is who
you are right now, and it is who you are meant to be.

Out of Touch

Open your eyes, look within. Are you satisfied with the
life you're living?

—Bob Marley

The notion of truth, above all, connotes honesty. Are you honest with yourself? Do you really know who you are and what you believe in? Or are you wearing masks just to please others? Can you look objectively at your situation, while still having confidence in yourself? Or are you playing victim, so others feel sorry for you? It's about being who you really are, fearlessly, rather than worrying what others think about you. When you're aligned with your truth, you don't change who you are to meet someone else's expectations; you change only to align better with your personal truth. (We'll cover aligning to your truth more in the next chapter on integrity.)

Brené Brown, in *The Gifts of Imperfection*, says, "Authenticity is the daily practice of letting go of who we think we're supposed to be and embracing who we are" (Brown, 2010). In the GRIT® model, authenticity combines both truth and integrity. Authenticity is aligning to your truth. But first we must start at truth so we have something to align to. This is where we begin to examine our beliefs and what is truly important to us. Throughout our lives, other people have influenced us. Along our path, many of us have lost ourselves; we're out of touch with who we truly are and what makes us genuinely happy. We've altered our behavior or made choices to please our parents, teachers, partners, or friends.

Most of us are not in the practice of taking the time to get to know ourselves. As Mark Twain said, "The two most important days in your life are the day you are born and the day you find out why." We're always in a hurry, trying to get everything accomplished, doing and being it all. We don't ever stop to ask ourselves if what we're doing is making us happy! When is the last time you reflected on what it is you really want out of life? We rarely pause and step back to decide if this is how we want to spend our time and energy. No wonder we feel empty, overwhelmed, unsatisfied with our accomplishments, and aimlessly seeking more out of life. And when we don't know our own truth and direction, it's pretty hard to successfully lead others. Try driving somewhere with no destination in mind. It would be hard to begin, let alone to keep going, without knowing your destination! How do we expect people to follow us?

Knowing our destination or where we want to be and what drives us—our intent—gives us direction and inspiration. Our intent is our meaning, our significance. Intent can be viewed as our overall life purpose or life force; in some contexts, then, intent is synonymous with truth. It is the truth we create. Intent can also be looked at as what is driving you in this single moment, why you are acting the way you are. Is it helpful or harmful? In both views, intent is related and connected.

When we are clear on our purpose or our meaning in life, our intent is positive and productive. When we are not clear—or perhaps we just aren't being mindful—our intent can be coming from a place of confusion or fear and can be harmful rather than helpful. For example, if I get frustrated and lash out, my intent may be to get even or punish. If I know and keep my truth in mind—for example, to help people become aware and make choices for themselves—then my intent will align to that and I won't lash out when I'm frustrated. I can use my frustration as an awareness for myself to align with my truth. My intent drives my actions and also helps me with awareness.

As leaders, when our intent is positive and helpful, the result is a productive, innovative, and enjoyable workforce. Our actions are a direct result of our intent; therefore, our intent is influencing what we are creating. If everything around you constantly seems negative, hold up a mirror and take a good hard look at yourself and your intent. What do you see? Are you operating out of fear? Is greed driving everything you do? Is there a feeling of scarcity or insecurity? Do you lack general trust of others? If so, what do you think this might be creating?

Intentional leaders have a positive and helpful intent. They are focused on helping develop and grow people. For example, when something becomes frustrating to an intentional leader, she remembers her purpose and her intent is to help, not hurt. Intentional leaders mindfully focus on the right issues and how to help the situation.

Where Does Our Truth Come From?

Can you remember who you were, before the world told you who you should be?

—Danielle LaPorte

When we are young, we are constantly told what we should and shouldn't believe by our parents, teachers, and other role models. At such a young age, most of us don't question what we're being told. We simply adopt these beliefs as our own. Until we become aware and start questioning those beliefs, most of us are not aware of what our truth is. We're just repeating what we've heard. Likewise, we're not consciously making choices; we're simply reacting to what happens to us. When something negative happens, we tend to look outside ourselves to blame it on something or someone else. We end up feeling trapped, frustrated, stressed, sad, helpless, angry, and/or apathetic.

Messages that we receive growing up stick with us, like a tape recorder. We've heard things like "It's hard work to make a good living" to "All people who are rich are greedy." Are those statements really true? Are they useful or helpful in any way? Until we erase those tapes, we'll keep living those lies. Yes, lies. I know that's a strong statement, but thinking about it as lies may encourage us to erase them more quickly.

We take whatever we hear, and we continue to repeat that to ourselves. We even create our own lies. It can actually be comical when you really start to listen to the voices in your head. Why would we say those things to ourselves? When you examine the statements, they're simply not true.

You can see how it happens. You hear something growing up, you attach to it subconsciously, and you repeat it, storing it on your tape recorder—usually without even thinking about it. We've all witnessed this in children who mirror mom and dad in words, behaviors, and even emotions, as young as two years old. These thoughts and beliefs can become deeply rooted emotionally, planted in our subconscious for later misuse.

Years ago, I volunteered to help teach entrepreneurial skills for an inner-city youth program. What a learning experience it was for me! It took a while for the students to warm up to me, but once they did—talk about being authentic! They openly shared their passions and their talents. I had so much fun learning about each one of them.

One day we were talking about turning some of those passions into goals and how that could create a better life. I had always assumed that a person would want to do better, and that given a chance, people would take it. Of course, I realized there would be some lack of confidence and maybe a little disbelief to deal with. I never imagined what I learned that day. My students told me that they believed that if they left and created a better life, it would be like dissing their families: "It's like we don't love them." They watched other family members leave in the past, either never to return or at odds if they did. The word was that those family members didn't respect what had been done for them. They were talked about as if they were selfish and thought they were better than everyone else. It had alienated them. To stay connected, to feel loved, these kids felt they couldn't leave. They felt very torn between staying where they were, and following their passion and making a better future for themselves.

Over the next few weeks, we spent hours questioning our thoughts and beliefs and talking about awareness, love, and choices. We agreed perhaps they could do it differently than others had in the past, and perhaps there was a way to be true to themselves and stay connected with the families they loved. Whatever these kids ended up choosing in life, at least now they would do it with awareness and positive intent. They will feel more empowered; they won't have to be victims.

We need to question our lies and beliefs and identify where they came from. Ask yourself, is it real for me still? Does it continue to serve me in a positive way, or was it a belief that served its purpose and needs to be renewed? Is there something emotional attaching me to that belief? We need to keep challenging our thoughts and beliefs to discover and remain true to ourselves.

Becoming Aware

What lies behind us and what lies before us are tiny matters compared to what lies within us.

—Ralph Waldo Emerson

Many of us find ourselves complaining about the job we have, the team we're stuck with, the lack of resources, the jerk of a boss, the idiots who know nothing in this company, and even our spouse. Really? That's how we want to spend this one life, complaining and feeling stuck? Think about it. Who chose to be in each one of those relationships? And who's choosing to stay? The choice is ultimately our own responsibility. It can seem like we just stumbled here, and sure, maybe a lot of our choices weren't made with awareness. It's true, we can't control the family we're born into or the neighborhood we're raised in. But at some point, we have to take ownership of our lives. As adults, it was our choice somewhere along the path that has gotten us here, and how we react to it is also our own choice. Awareness is the first step toward discovering our truth.

Sometimes we become aware just by luck, or so it seems. Something happens, and you get an aha moment. Other times, perhaps someone does or says something that inspires you to take a good objective look at yourself. Maybe it's not a pleasant experience, but it may bring awareness. I suppose this is what happened with my 7 A.M. wake-up call!

At times, there may be something that's blocking you from getting to your truth, and you may not even realize it. In other words, you don't know what you don't know. You just know you're not happy, or not fulfilled, or something is just not feeling right. You can use your emotions to help you become aware.

If we pay attention to how we are feeling, we can learn a lot about ourselves. I remember being stuck in a construction zone one day as I was racing to the post office to mail an important document, about 10 minutes before it closed. I felt myself becoming very impatient and irritated as I watched while no one was allowed to cross into the post office. They were painting the lines on the road. As I watched the seconds tick by, I could feel my anxiety growing. Because I had been practicing paying attention to my emotions, I quickly noticed this, took a deep breath, and realized the workers weren't deliberately keeping me from crossing the street. I smiled at the man holding the flag and asked if there was any way to get me into the post office in the next 5 minutes before it closed. I'm pretty sure that had I been irritated and short with him, he would not have so eagerly looked for a solution for me and helped me meet my deadline that day.

Recognizing that I had the power to choose a different response changed my perspective and allowed a successful resolution to my dilemma, while staying true to myself. It's about not allowing a situation to change us, and we end up doing something we regret. With mindful awareness, I also learned more about my overall self. Waiting until the last minute seemed to be a pattern of behavior with me. Our emotions are a great awareness tool.

The problem is that most of us have been taught to stuff down our emotions. They can be uncomfortable, so we avoid them or resist them. I'm not saying we should all feel free to express whatever we are feeling whenever we want. That might not be very respectful to others around us, especially in the workplace. But if we can just pay attention to an emotion as we feel it, that's a start. Think of your emotions as a tool to help you be aware. The next time you feel frustrated, stop and ask yourself, "What's going on with me right now? Why am I finding this situation so stressful?" What we tend to do is point away from ourselves and blame it on something external. It's not to say that stuff doesn't happen, but we know it's more about how we react to it. If we can turn the incident into an opportunity to examine why we're reacting, we may discover more about ourselves.

Some of us would rather avoid our truth. It can be uncomfortable to start poking around in there. Who knows what we might stumble upon and then have to deal with! You may be hesitant to open that can of worms. But if we don't take the time to self-reflect, then we're leaving our lives, happiness, and future up to sheer luck. Think about it: This is your one shot at this life! Each one of us has a lot more control over our lives than we typically give ourselves credit for. With some time spent on getting to know our truth and choosing what we want in order to align with our truth, we can create the experiences we want, therefore living the life we're intended to live.

Prevent Ego from Interfering

He who is in the thickest fog blows his own horn.
—Anonymous

There may be people who are just not willing to self-reflect and look objectively at themselves—that's the reality of it. We need to respect where they are and their choices. If we are feeling too responsible for someone else's happiness, we need to hold up the mirror, ask ourselves why, and keep asking until we really discover our reason, our truth. Could it be our ego? Perhaps we're not respecting their journey and allowing them the opportunity for awareness?

Our egos are just the social mask we wear. Our egos seek approval. It's not really our true self, the core of who we are. Our ego is driven by fear. It wants power and control. Our true self is the perfect balance of confidence and humility, not controlled by fear.

Our egos have an interesting impact on our perception of our truth, causing us sometimes to feel too self-assured and sometimes not assured enough. This can certainly get in the way of recognizing our truth. On the one hand, when you're too self-assured, you might think you already know something, you attach to that, and it's very difficult to remain open to other possibilities. On the other hand, when you're not assured enough, you might keep second-guessing yourself. If we acknowledge our ego is there and admit what it might be doing, we can prevent it from getting in the way of our truth.

There Are Many Paths to Find Your Truth

Over every mountain there is a path, although it may not be seen from the valley.

—Theodore Roethke

With mindful awareness, we may be able to discover our truth on our own. We can schedule time to reflect, be still, and pay attention to our feelings, emotions, thoughts, beliefs, and actions. Practicing silence helps us find our true selves. All the noise, the voices, the television, the opinions, the books, the music—they drown out who we really are, and we lose touch. Not that you should stop these things completely, although minimizing some would no doubt benefit you, but schedule some quiet time to just be.

We can practice being present in the moment to quiet our minds. Our minds are typically in one of two places: in the future or in the past. We're either worrying about what we need to do or regretting what we've done. It's all right to take a quick trip to the future and consider your goals and aspirations, or to take a quick trip to the past to learn from it, but it becomes a problem when we stay in either place too long. Then our minds are too busy to find our truth. We forget about the present moment. We neglect to enjoy ourselves in the here and now.

There are things we can do to practice present moment awareness. For example, while brushing your teeth, think only of brushing your teeth. How the bristles feel on each tooth, spending the same amount of time on each tooth, paying attention to the direction you brush—you get the picture. It's actually pretty difficult to do because it's an activity that doesn't take thought, so we tend to let our minds run wild. When you catch yourself thinking of something else, bring your mind back to your teeth. This is not to say you shouldn't brush your teeth while thinking of other things—it's just a great example of how you can practice being present in the moment.

Not judging things can also quiet your mind and help you find your truth. We spend so much time with our opinions, such as this is good or bad, right or wrong, healthy or not, pretty or ugly. We're in such a habit of doing this we don't even realize it. Just try an hour or two of not judging anything. As you practice, it gets easier. You're training your mind to be quiet, so the real you can be heard. All the judgments we make keep our minds so busy and feed our ego, so we don't really know the real truth. Think of being still, like a calm lake. When you toss a pebble in (your intention), you can see it ripple and spread. But if we're not still, if we're like a roaring turbulent water, even if you toss in a boulder, you won't see the ripple. So even if you're screaming for something you want, it won't happen.

Yoga is a great way to practice being present in the moment. As we practice being still and focused, it helps us clear our minds and can help us get to our truths. After yoga, I feel a lot less stressed. I'm more focused, creative, and productive. I feel like I'm exactly where I'm supposed to be. Others may prefer activities like fishing, golfing, skiing, or sewing, for example. The key is how you feel during and after the activity. If you are frustrated, annoyed, overwhelmed, or feeling any other negative emotion, it may not be helping you and therefore is not a mind-quieting activity. If it's not, but you really want to continue the activity, you can learn to quiet your mind during this time; it's kind of like the chicken before the egg syndrome. Some activities naturally help us be present; others we need to practice being present while in the activity.

There are many inspirational authors who can help us to discover our truth through their books, such as Eckhardt Tolle, Wayne Dyer, Deepak Chopra, Don Miguel Ruiz, Brené Brown, Byron Katie, and Dan Millman.

Another way to help you discover your purpose is attending personal retreats. One of my favorite retreats has been with Don Miguel Ruiz, who wrote *The Four Agreements* (Ruiz, 1997). During the retreat, many guided activities helped us be present in the moment, to not judge, to accept ourselves, and ultimately helped us be more aware of our truths.

Personality type assessment tools are helpful to discover our preferences and tendencies and, when used appropriately, can be very beneficial in a workplace. I've used Wiley's DiSC® Assessment for many years in almost every training program. It's an efficient and effective way for team members to understand and appreciate each other. In essence, we begin with an awareness of our truth—behavioral strengths and limitations. Through sharing our individual truths with our team, we then take it to a level of working effectively together, based on those truths.

DiSC® is grounded in William Marston's 1930s model, with Dominance, Influence, Steadiness, and Conscientiousness representing the four behavioral styles. Basically, it is about a person's preferences or tendencies, and it's very useful for us to understand our own and then be able to adapt to effectively interact and communicate with others. The best way to experience DiSC® is to take the assessment yourself (contact us at info@unlimitedcoaching.com).

Figure 2.1 shows the styles and some of the general characteristics of each.

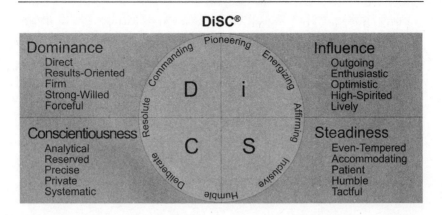

Figure 2.1. The Four Styles of DiSC®

And sometimes, it just takes time, friends, and even professional help to be objective so that you can find your truth.

Look Objectively

Freedom is knowing who you really are.

—Linda Thomson

Awareness of our own truth is powerful. It's the beginning of freedom, happiness, and success! However, when you discover a truth about yourself, you may need to proceed with caution. Many people have a tendency to be negative when recognizing a truth about themselves. Once uncovered, they beat themselves up, either for actually being that way or for not recognizing it sooner! For example, I shared in Chapter 1 how I became aware of my negative attitude, with the help of our overly cheerful receptionist. When I think back, I probably spent a bit of time beating myself up over acting that way. It's what we do—we discover something we think should be different about ourselves, and we agonize over it. That actually keeps us there longer. It's better to just move on, rather than hang there and fixate on it.

That's exactly what Dan was doing when I began coaching him. In his leadership role, Dan was expected to be open and receptive to his team. His 360 feedback report indicated that his team, as well as his boss, perceived he was not. Dan spent a lot of time making excuses for it, and then he was upset that it took the 360 assessment for him to be aware of it! We laughed about that later. Once Dan understood the value of being objective, he moved on and we began our work.

Look at your situation objectively. Accept where you are. When we accept our situation rather than resist it, we can be open rather than closed. Resistance causes us to put even more focus on what we don't want, and it persists. Acceptance helps us to be able to move on. The cool thing is that, with awareness and acceptance, you now have the power to change something—if you want to. Be grateful for the experience. This awareness is helping you become who you long to be.

It's Your Choice

Be happy, or be stupid.

—Don Miguel Ruiz

Once you're aware, you have choice. It's that simple. Just imagine being miserable every single day at work. Is this how you want to be spending your time? Being miserable, at all, anywhere? Is it really working? Is that really your truth? I highly doubt it. Some people don't believe it's possible to be happy; they are addicted to suffering. After all, a lot of us believe you have to suffer to make money. Isn't that a belief in being miserable? Maybe somewhere deep down, for some reason, we don't think we deserve to be happy. Perhaps being miserable and suffering gets attention, and that attention fills a need. So while "Be happy, or be stupid" is simple in concept, it may take practice in awareness to help us make this choice.

Drama can be addictive, and most people who are drama addicts don't even realize it. Until they become aware and figure out why (aha, the truth!), they will not know that they can choose happiness. It's difficult for them to see the benefit because they can't even see that they are stuck. Maybe their path is just different, and maybe they have more to experience before they can make a shift. And some people may never shift, in which case we need to respect where they are. After all, we can't fully know a person's path or their truth. (We'll expand more in Chapter 4 on respect.)

When you know your truth, you have clarity, and you're more confident. You make decisions that align with what's important to you. It's much easier to know if a particular situation is right, if a person is right, or if a job is the best fit when you are clear on your truth and have the courage to stay true to yourself. As Shakespeare said, "To thine own self be true." You trust yourself and your judgment. You don't constantly second-guess your situation, your relationship, your sanity! You're not continually doubting yourself or making choices to please others. Knowing your truth makes it easier to choose whether to stay in a relationship or leave, be it a bad marriage or a dysfunctional work environment.

Sometimes we have competing priorities. Decision making then becomes a question of what is most important to you. Consider the adolescents who participated in the inner-city youth entrepreneurial program and the competing priorities they had: They felt torn between their family's love and acceptance and the possibility of a future with more security and less tragedy. Without awareness and questioning, we may never be able to see the competing priorities and gain clarity. We might end up just reacting and feeling stuck like a victim.

Take the time to rank-order your priorities. This will help you consider your choices and more efficiently and effectively make decisions. Rather than think *either-or*, this allows you to consider *how* you can get the results you want. When we know what's most important to us, in what order, we can use that knowledge to guide our decisions.

When we discover our truth and align our decisions with our truth, we learn to trust in ourselves again. We trust our intuition more. We go with our gut instead of overanalyzing and overthinking everything. It's not that we don't use our logic. We balance the two. Our logic and intuition can work in harmony together. Even Albert Einstein said, "I believe in intuitions and inspirations . . . . I sometimes FEEL that I am right. I do not KNOW that I am."

Most definitions of intuition include a component of both self-awareness and direct knowledge. The key is awareness—knowing yourself and trusting that instinctual feeling. In a study by W. H. Agor, *The Logic of Intuition*, it was found that many executives have admitted to relying on intuition when making some of their most successful decisions. When we can rely on our intuition, decision making is more efficient and reliable.

Change Your Story

Remember, no matter where you go, there you are.

—Confucius

As we all know, reputations are easily created and much harder to change. Reputations are not your truth; they are perceptions that other people have about you. People latch onto an image, and it sticks. It is said that it takes only seven seconds to make a first impression. We then look for things to support this image. To change our reputation, it starts with changing our own story. Then, of course, we have to align our actions, but it will be much more effective if we are confident in our beliefs about ourselves first.

Perhaps as you begin your search for your truth, you uncover some thoughts or beliefs you're not happy about. Maybe those thoughts or beliefs have led to actions or behaviors that you don't want to continue doing anymore. Happiness is the best gauge. Yes, I know, it sounds like such a cliché. But happiness really is what it's about. It either works for you or it doesn't. Do you like the consequences you're getting, or not? It boils down to how you feel. That is how you'll know if you are aligning to your truth or if you want to make a change.

For example, perhaps you've been blunt, insensitive, or even verbally abusive in your role as a leader. In other words, you have a reputation as a jerk. In a sense, you believe it does take being a jerk to get things done, and so you see yourself as that jerk. Maybe you wouldn't use the same word, but you can admit it's the same thing and that your actions are responsible for this reputation. You also realize that it is your thoughts and beliefs that have prompted your actions. If you can change your thoughts about what it takes to lead successfully, and believe that people want to follow someone who is authentic and caring yet direct and fair, you can change your actions and your reputation.

If you don't believe it is true that people will be more productive, creative, and efficient with a leader who is authentic, caring, direct, and fair, then you will not change your actions, and you will not see yourself in that image. You will not change your story, and if you do happen to change your behaviors, perhaps because your boss has insisted, it won't last. You'll go back to old habits and, in time, to being the jerk. In this case, the work that needs to be done is around changing your thoughts and beliefs, and you may need evidence to help you see and believe what it takes to be a successful leader. This book is a great start. A leadership course and other books can help, too.

What Do You Want in Life?

Find something you're passionate about and keep tremen-
dously interested in it.

—Julia Child

Your biggest challenge with truth might be to discover what you really want in life. As Dr. Seuss said in *Oh, the Places You'll Go!* (Seuss 1960) "Simple it's not, I'm afraid you will find, for a mind maker-upper to make up his mind." It's not always clear where we want to go. Ironically, sometimes you just need to let go of the need to know where you're going. When we let go, things flow. Similar to when you can't think of a song although it's on the tip of your tongue. As soon as you give up trying to remember it, it comes to you.

Relax and pay more attention to how you're feeling. What resonates with you can point you in the direction of your passions (your truth). Don't force it. You'll cause resistance. It's okay not to know everything. Understand that you don't have to have the total picture in focus to find your truth. Your truth at this moment is that you are where you are. Be good to yourself about where you are. Give yourself permission to take your time to figure it out. Don't be in such a hurry. Sometimes it's simply patience that we need. As I've been teaching my 3-year-old grandson, patience is waiting and being happy. The message we often get about being patient is negative—someone yelling at us to be patient. Practice being present in the moment to help you with patience, and you will find that you get all the time you need.

Once you are clear on what you want, enjoy conjuring up a picture and a feeling of how it will be when you're there. For the jerk who wants to be a successful leader, it's seeing yourself less stressed, getting a lot more done, people respecting you, and you're actually enjoying yourself. Visualize it. Dream about it.

Sense it. Feel it. There's real power in being able to visualize a future image. We trick our minds into believing we are already that image, and we begin to act that way.

While you're visualizing, pay close attention to your thoughts and beliefs. Do you believe that you can change? Do you believe in yourself and that if you really want something, and you really focus on it, you can make it happen? Are your thoughts supporting it, or are the voices denying it? Often we need to work on changing our thoughts and beliefs.

Change Your Thoughts

All that you achieve and all that you fail to achieve is the direct result of your own thoughts.

—James Allen

Similar to changing your story, many people don't realize that you really can control your thoughts. And if your thoughts are negative all the time, well, garbage in, garbage out, right? Consider how negative thoughts might be impacting you. If you are putting in unhealthy thoughts, food, or anything else for that matter, what can you expect as a consequence? Our thoughts are something we can manage and take care of. Consider this—would you leave your toddler unattended to do whatever he wanted? Then why would you let your thoughts wander negatively? They are both dangerous situations. You can guide your thoughts in a better direction if you are aware of them.

It's those voices in your head. Start paying attention to what they are saying. Just kind of stalk yourself for a while to notice the message your voices are telling you. As soon as you catch yourself being a Debbie Downer, for example, coax your mind back. Refrain from judging it—just steer it back onto the road of positive thinking.

Often it takes rewiring our subconscious mind to get it to think differently, and consequently, we will feel and act differently. Positive affirmations, or mantras, are an effective way to do this. Take one of the messages in your head that you'd like to change, and turn it into an opposite and positive statement. For example, "I have to work so hard and suffer to make a good living" becomes "I work smart and enjoy my time, and I make a better living this way." If you repeat this phrase often enough, your subconscious will replace the older negative statement with this newer, more positive version.

Our subconscious mind plays a major role in our actions because this is where all our thoughts and beliefs are stored. The subconscious mind influences the conscious mind. The good news is that it takes a small investment of time to work on changing the subconscious mind. It has been discovered through research on our thoughts and dreams that the last 15 minutes before we go to sleep greatly affects our dreams. Whatever we are thinking about gets played over in our minds 15 to 17 times. So you are essentially brainwashing yourself! If indeed we are brainwashing ourselves, why not make it a positive experience? Wayne Dyer says to "marinate" in your mind as you sleep. Give yourself a dose of positivity every night!

I know by the way I feel in the morning if I need to change something I did the night before. Occasionally I'll get into a habit of falling asleep with the TV or radio on, and all that crap is imprinting my brain all night. As soon as I'm aware that I feel tired and not really inspired in the morning, I know I need to make a change in my nighttime routine. Just reading something positive, engaging in a great conversation, or spending quality time with someone you love can make a big difference. I feel better. I'm not positive there's a correlation, but it sure seems like I need less sleep when I focus on the positive things before going to bed.

The Impact of Truth

That which is false troubles the heart, but truth brings joyous tranquility.

—Rumi

Consider how all of this affects a workplace. A group of people are placed together to be productive, to create something. As we know, we each carry our own baggage to work every day. When we interact with others, the baggage comes out in ways that people misunderstand, resulting in turf wars, miscommunications, lack of trust, avoidance of accountability, abuse, condescending attitudes, elitism, and gossip.

No one but you can know what your truth is and what baggage you're carrying today. Your boss may know what you're capable of in the past, but he can't know if that's your truth right now. And your truth may not look the same from one moment to the next or to the next person. Everyone's personal truth is different on different days, at different times. You might be affected physically, emotionally, or mentally, for better or worse. Your output will depend on whether you are feeling happy, angry, sad, ill, or tired. If you overdo it, you may end up depleting yourself, so that your output on the task at hand or the next one may not be what you are normally capable of. This can also lead to feelings of failure, and you end up performing subpar to what you normally would.

When you know your own truth, you know what you are capable of in any given moment. For example, the quality of your work may vary, but you do the best you can do, in each moment, under the circumstances, which are always changing. If you expect yourself to be perfect by someone else's standards (someone else judging you), you are no longer in your own truth.

Similarly, if you expect others to be your definition of perfect for them, you'll certainly be disappointed.

When you are authentic, you are creating what you are capable of, nothing more, nothing less. At the same time, when you take actions that align to your truth—managing your thoughts and beliefs, not allowing garbage in—you stay closer to your truth.

Consider who you are in your role at home, in your social circle, at work—do you really know yourself? Do you know what makes you happy? Have you chosen the people, the places, the career that fits you? Are you taking full responsibility for where you are right now (and not blaming or complaining)? Maybe you've found yourself in a very negative, toxic work environment. You might be thinking, "I chose this job, but I certainly didn't choose to work with these idiots." It's true, we don't always know what will result from the choices we make. But we do know that we can always make different choices. Maybe not leave the instant you discover it's the wrong environment for you, but take ownership that you are the one who chose to be here, and you can choose to get yourself out of it. It may take time to figure this out and make the next choice for yourself. You might decide to stay and choose to look at it differently because there are different priorities for you right now. Your truth might be, you have a family to take care of and bills to pay. And still, it boils down to choice. If you are clear on your priorities, your truth, and your intent, you'll continue to make decisions that align for you. You'll feel empowered rather than victimized.

A few years back, a good friend packed up his family and moved to an area that was better for them as a multicultural family. Joe had sought out a well-paying job in the field he loved and found a neighborhood that proved to be perfect for them. All was well, until he was laid off. Now what? Joe searched for months for another job in the same area, to no avail. With the agreement of his wife and children, they chose to move to another state and start over. They moved to a beautiful neighborhood and a comfortable home with an inground swimming pool and many great amenities. However, the neighborhood was not what they expected. And the job turned out to be about the worst corporate culture he could ever have imagined. Since I've known Joe, he has always been aware of his priorities and aligned to them. In this situation, he had done his best to do just that. But it doesn't always turn out as one imagines, and once we discover it's not what we want, it's time to make new choices. And that's exactly what Joe did. It wasn't practical for him to quit and move instantly, but over time, he found a new job, back near their old neighborhood, and within a year Joe and his family moved and he was settling into the new company and culture. Just imagine, he and his family could have suffered for years in that situation, had he not chosen to align to his priorities and make a change. In any situation, with an awareness of our truth, we will be clear on our priorities and align our choices, which will result in efficiency, productivity, satisfaction, and happiness in our lives.

Finding your truth is not a one-time, fix-all, never have to work on any of it again kind of thing. As you evolve and grow, your truth will evolve and grow. If we trust our emotions and use them as an indicator of when we are aligning with our truth, we can make choices. *We will be free* to live the life we were meant to. And then we can authentically lead others.

Before you venture into Chapter 3, take some time to reflect.

What SHIFT Will You Make?

Scan the chapter. List the topics that resonated with you.

_____

_____

Hone in on one or two areas that will make the biggest impact for you.

_____

_____

Imagine the impact. Why is this important? How will you feel when you've accomplished this?

_____

_____

Figure out your plan and how you will stay on track.

_____

_____

Take action. Start now. Schedule it now, and include your follow-up.

_____

_____

Enjoy! Remember to choose to be happy, every step of the way!

_____

_____

References

Angor, W., (1986). The Logic of Intuition. Organizational Dynamics, Vol. 14 (3), PP. 5–18.

Brown, B. (2010). _The Gifts of Imperfection: Let go of who you think you're supposed to be and embrace who you are._ Center City, Minnesota: Hazelden Publishing.

Ruiz, D. M. (1997). _The Four Agreements: A practical guide to personal freedom._ San Rafael, California: Amber-Allen Publishing, Inc.

Seuss (1960). Oh the Places You'll Go. New York, New York: Random House Children's Books.

● CHAPTER THREE

INTEGRITY—ALIGNING TO YOUR TRUTH

Be yourself—everyone else is already taken.

—Oscar Wilde

I was recently talking with a client who had missed her daughter's dance rehearsal. She felt terrible. I know this client pretty well; we've been working on this pattern of behavior for a little while. It's very tough for her to break. While she knows intellectually that her daughter is more important than work, she has been in the habit of making decisions that don't align to that. She's beginning to recognize this pattern and take ownership, which has been the hardest step for her. She's noticing the direct link to her daughter's behavior and other negative results—based on her decisions and actions. For example, she's realizing that in blaming her ex-husband, she was taking the responsibility off

herself. Not to say that he didn't have a part to play,
but she realized that it was distracting her from
taking full responsibility for her own actions. She
used to think, "Wow, how did I get here? Why is this
happening to me?" Now she can trace what choices
she has made and see the connections clearly. She
knows when her actions are not aligning to her truth.

Think back to a time when you did something because someone else wanted you to, even though you really didn't want
to do it. You said yes to a project that you didn't have time for,
or you agreed to have that tough conversation with a coworker
that the boss should have had. Or maybe you gave up an important personal commitment for work. What was your energy level
like? What were you feeling? For most of us, our energy level is
low, and there's usually some negative emotion involved. We feel
overwhelmed, drained, and resentful. If we pay attention to this,
we'll know when we are not in integrity.

Integrity is aligning your actions with your truth. If you look
up the definition of *integrity*, you'll see it's about honesty and
moral character, being whole or complete, and being unimpaired
or perfect. In GRIT®, integrity is about being in alignment with
your truth, and in that context, we are looking at it as being
whole, complete, or balanced. You are doing the things that you
say are important to you, in a balanced way. Integrity is also
about being unimpaired in the sense that your actions line up
perfectly to your truth, so you're not broken or impaired. When
it comes to the part on perfection, we aren't talking about an
unattainable perfection that many people stress over (someone
else's definition of perfection); we're talking about doing your
best to remain true to yourself and accepting that as perfection.

If we don't take the time to reflect on what's important to us,
as we discovered in Chapter 2, we won't know what actions to
take. We won't know if the choice we are making in this moment
aligns. We'll most likely end up thinking, "How the heck did this

happen?" or maybe even feeling like "Why is this happening to me?" The only way the chaos will stop is when we start making different choices—choices that align to our truth. Being in integrity is about aligning our choices and our actions to our truth.

Awareness, Intent, Attention

We judge ourselves by our intentions and others by their behavior.

—Stephen M. R. Covey

We know from Chapter 2 that without awareness, we won't feel empowered to make a difference in our own lives. If we are aware of our intent, we will know what is driving our actions, and it will help align us to our truth. Then we can choose where to focus our attention, as the Triangle of Intent illustrates (see Figure 3.1).

Intent extends from truth to integrity. It is the driving force that guides our focus and attention, which directly impacts our behavior. It is possible to be aware of and change our intent in

ATTENTION

INTENT

AWARENESS

Figure 3.1. Triangle of Intent

any single moment, just by asking ourselves, "Is it helpful or harmful? Is it positive or negative?" As discussed in Chapter 2, intent can be looked at as your life force or life purpose, and it can also be viewed as what drives you in this single moment (which, of course, is linked to your life purpose). But even when you don't know your life purpose, you can look at your intent in this moment and align it positively rather than negatively.

Intent is internal, and people may not be aware of your intent; they only see your behavior. We judge each other on behavior, not on intent. If we are aware, we will ensure that our behavior aligns with our intent.

When I was rushing to the post office that day the lines were being painted on the street and I couldn't drive over it, my feelings of frustration and anxiety were my awareness. Without awareness, I would have behaved very differently, yelling or just not asking in a helpful way. By paying attention to my emotions, I could be mindful of my intent and focus my attention on a solution rather than just the problem. When I communicated in a positive manner and even used a little humor, the construction workers could hear me better. They were more inspired to help me, finding a large piece of cardboard to lay over the wet paint so I could get to the post office on time.

Imagine how it could have gone down, had I been out of integrity. I yell or say something sarcastic, or I get stressed and say nothing at all. They roll their eyes or ignore me because of the negative energy emitting from my car. I miss the post office deadline. I blame them. And the vicious cycle continues. When I react negatively and do something I regret, I'm not in integrity. That is not who I really am at my core; I know I am a positive, compassionate person. I allowed something or someone to get me off track. We know when we're not in integrity by the way we feel.

As a manager, if your intent is to help your people, and you believe that delegating work to an employee helps him or her learn and develop, you won't hold on to too much work. You won't deny your people the opportunity. You will give the appropriate tasks to the appropriate people and not victimize yourself by taking it all on. When you pay attention to the frustration you are feeling, you can reflect inward to see where your intent is, realizing that if you hold on to that work, you will not be in alignment with your truth. It's not helping either one of you.

The good news is that it only takes practice in awareness to make this happen. Awareness allows us the opportunity to look objectively, understand where our intent is, and shift it if necessary. Like anything else—learning to walk, ride a bike, swim, play the drums, be a great leader—we need to pay some attention to it, and do it. Integrity takes practice. Life is about practice. Awareness and intent help us focus on what to practice.

As with everything in life, it's a choice what you focus on and practice—even your thoughts! Again, that's why knowing our truth is so important. Then we can choose the thoughts and beliefs we want, and our practice will line up to that!

Our feelings are really good at telling us when we're not in integrity with ourselves. By paying attention to our emotions and our physiological state, we can become aware of when it may be time to change our behavior and align with our truth. But what most of us do when we experience an emotion is look outside of ourselves for the cause. He did this to me, or she made me unhappy. We do this rather than looking inside and seeing what's going on with us!

Easier said than done! We're not in a habit of paying attention to our emotions and then holding up a mirror. It's easier to look at the world around us and blame it on something out there. It's not to say that stuff doesn't happen. It's how we react to it that's important.

Imagine if we could identify that emotional feeling *before* we took action? We could do a gut check and ask ourselves before we reacted, "Does this align with my priorities? Is this the right choice for me right now? Where is my intent?" Imagine the torment we could avoid.

It's powerful to be able to choose where to focus your attention. Consider the basic choice of positive or negative; for example, is the glass half empty or half full? We can choose to focus on the positive things, or we can let ourselves be consumed by the negative.

This isn't to say that we would ignore the negative things; it's simply to say that we can choose where to focus our attention and how we react. We can pick our battles. Often, we are not even aware of where our attention is focused. It becomes habitual, and soon we're focusing on the negative way more than the positive, piling on to the negative situation. A perfect example of this is negative gossip. When you find yourself in that situation, think about being gasoline or water on the fire. You can be gasoline and add to the gossip, or you can be water and put it out.

Whatever we focus our attention on, we will naturally look for supporting facts. For example, have you ever noticed when you buy a new car, all of a sudden so many people have the same car? So many more of those cars seem to be on the road now! We may even believe that everyone copied us by purchasing the same car. In actuality, we just weren't focused on that model car before and didn't notice all of those cars out there. We're more in tune to that model car now, so we focus on that.

Therefore, if we're clear on what we want, we can focus and look for facts to support it. When we know what we want from ourselves, from our teams, from our families and friends, we can focus our attention there. We'll start to believe in it. We can then choose to focus on the thoughts, facts, activities, and behaviors that support the positive behavior we seek. Often we have a tendency to focus on what we don't want, and as Carl Jung said, "What we resist, persists." When we look for positive, we will experience positive; when we look for negative, we will experience negative. For example, if you look for mistakes and imperfections, you'll find many. If you look for learning experiences and different options, that is what you'll get.

The Triangle of Intent helps illustrate this. If you focus on something you don't want, you are giving more attention and energy to it. It will persist! Furthermore, resisting your truth causes stress. We're no longer in integrity when we're stressed because we're going against ourselves.

Take reputations, for example. We talked about changing our story in Chapter 2. When you know what you want to be, and you know where you currently are, then you simply look at what behaviors you need to change. Focus on those behaviors, not the ones you don't want anymore. Practice. It's true that it can be challenging when others still have that old image of you burned on their brains. To change perceptions, you might have to help them see the new you by bringing their attention to the facts that support the new you. Verbalize your intent. Sure, it can feel vulnerable, but it can also be very liberating, and it will help you stay aligned.

Imagine if you could believe in your people and trust them to succeed—you could look for facts to support their success rather than look for facts to support their dysfunction. This will in turn influence the way you react to people, and it has a direct impact on their behavior.

Your Actions Influence Others

Think twice before you speak, because your words and influence will plant the seed of either success or failure in the mind of another.

—Napoleon Hill

The reality is we're not responsible for other people's behaviors, but we do have an influence. Leadership is all about influence. Whether we want to or not, we are influencing people. In our formal leadership roles as managers and even parents, it is our responsibility to help others perform to their best and grow. It's important to know where to focus our attention. Similar to tending a garden, provide the best soil, sunlight, and attention, and you will reap the best harvest.

Our communication certainly has an influence on others. Since your truth and your intent is internal, and people can't mind read, it is your responsibility to communicate your truth, first to yourself and then to the people around you. When we are in integrity, our communication is clear. We say what we need to say. We don't beat around the bush. We say it in a way that we feel will be most helpful—but we say it.

However, it's up to you to decide what and how much to share, based on your priorities, respect for yourself, and respect for others. It's not about sharing everything with everyone. You have a right to your own privacy, and it's not always beneficial or respectful to share certain information. In Chapter 8, we'll explore communication and the use of filters.

To stay in integrity, we need to say no when something doesn't align. If we don't say no, and we take action that is not aligned, then we will be out of integrity. Something else will suffer. Or we might end up not being able to deliver on what we've said yes to, and this, too, will get us out of integrity. Saying no is essential to keeping on track with our priorities. We just need to respect others and say no the best we can. We delve into methods of saying no in Chapter 9.

What comes out of our mouths is a direct reflection of how we feel about ourselves. When our tone is defensive, it's typically an indication that we're fearful of something; we're protecting ourselves; we're trying to avoid something. When we're uncomfortable with saying what we really need or want to say, we might mask it with sarcasm, or we may blow up and yell at someone. The result we get is the opposite of what we want.

Our intent is generally that we want someone to become aware and change. When we don't communicate with integrity, typically a person either does not get it and does not change or gets it, gets mad, and does not change. It's counterproductive because you've created a difficult communication scenario. This sets up an even greater barrier for the other person to be direct and honest. In the rare occasion that a person does have the courage to ask what you mean, your typical reaction is to laugh it off and be even less direct, causing more confusion. Chapters 8 and 9 help us to craft our message in a way that gets the meaning across and to say what we need to say.

One of the greatest ways we influence others is by our own actions. What are we doing that other people will imitate? Josh Shipp, a former at-risk foster kid turned teen advocate (and nicknamed the teen whisperer) has been spreading the message that "Your imperfections make you human and your humanity makes you influential." Being authentic and real, staying aligned to your truth, will be seen in your actions. We've all heard it—our actions speak louder than words. Telling others what to do but not doing it yourself sends the wrong message. Do we walk the talk? Do we practice what we preach?

Dorothy Nolte's *Children Learn What They Live* is a perfect illustration of living in integrity and realizing the impact we have on others. It's not only in childhood that we can make an impact. We can use this in our daily lives and in our role as leaders. Just substitute the word *people* in place of *children*.

> If children live with criticism, they learn to condemn.
>
> If children live with hostility, they learn to fight.
>
> If children live with fear, they learn to be apprehensive.
>
> If children live with pity, they learn to feel sorry for themselves.
>
> If children live with ridicule, they learn to feel shy.

If children live with jealousy, they learn to feel envy.

If children live with shame, they learn to feel guilty.

If children live with encouragement, they learn confidence.

If children live with tolerance, they learn patience.

If children live with praise, they learn appreciation.

If children live with acceptance, they learn to love.

If children live with approval, they learn to like themselves.

If children live with recognition, they learn it is good to have a goal.

If children live with sharing, they learn generosity.

If children live with honesty, they learn truthfulness.

If children live with fairness, they learn justice.

If children live with kindness and consideration, they learn respect.

If children live with security, they learn to have faith in themselves and in those about them.

If children live with friendliness, they learn the world is a nice place in which to live.

—(Nolte, 1972)

When there's congruity in what we say and what we do, people will trust us. They will learn from us. They will follow us.

We make choices every minute of every day. These choices affect our lives. It is our choices, more than anything else, that are creating the experiences we are having. If we really know and understand our priorities in life, and we have our thoughts and beliefs aligned, we can make the choices that align to our truth, and then we will be in Integrity. And then we will be happy.

Revisit your top priorities in life from Chapter 2. Maybe they're things like health, family, friends, career, and fun. As we know, it's different for each of us. Whatever those priorities are, it's important for us to ask ourselves if we are aligning our activities to them—or are we getting sidetracked by doing busywork or maybe just reacting to anything that comes at us? It can certainly be challenging today with all the options. It's very easy to get distracted, and without even realizing it, we are doing something that isn't aligned to what we say is important.

Time *Can* Be On Your Side

Time is what we want most, but what we use worst.

—William Tell

Then there's the issue of so much to do and so little time! Many of us can relate to this feeling. But we all get the same amount of time in a day, don't we? It has a lot more to do with how we manage ourselves—the choices we make and how we use the time. Are we aligning to the most important things? Or are we allowing things to hook our attention, things that aren't really priorities, but simply distractions? Some of us are more prone to getting distracted than others, and some of us are so rigid we rarely get distracted, but we also don't balance enough flexibility to be open to something new or spontaneous, causing us to miss some of life's opportunities. That's why it's so important to know ourselves so we can be prepared and be disciplined when necessary. If we know the areas where we need to focus more energy, we can put our attention there.

For some of us, we're in the habit of being busy. Maybe this started because we believe to be successful, we must be busy, and we've practiced being busy so much it has become second nature. Even though we might now believe that a person can be very successful without being so busy, and we believe that it's actually a smarter way to be, our actions are still not aligning. We continue to act busy. Have you ever noticed it? You are going to see a friend or do something that you really don't need to be in a hurry for, but you're rushing around as if you are in a hurry. We get used to acting a certain way; we're not being mindful of what action is really needed in each particular situation.

Choices That Keep Us Whole

In nature, there are neither awards nor punishments— there are consequences.

—Robert G. Ingersoll

When we know our truth and live by it, we are in integrity with ourselves. An element of being in integrity includes being whole, being complete, and being balanced. We make the right choices for ourselves, from basic needs like the amount of sleep and what foods we eat, to how to handle more challenging work- place issues. This includes making the right choices to take care of ourselves. Each of us is different, so we need to know our- selves and what we need, and then give ourselves what we need. For example, I may require seven hours of sleep, eight glasses of water, and five days of exercise. Someone else could be great on five hours of sleep and maybe more water and less exercise. It's one thing to know what we need (and know our truth); it's another thing to actually practice it. When we don't get the sleep we need, we are tired and make rash decisions, perhaps the wrong food to eat. Then we're too tired to exercise. Then we don't have the energy we need. Then we make more rash decisions. Then we lash out at someone because we are irritable, and then we blame it on them, and, well, you can see the snowball effect! Ask yourself, am I allocating the right amounts of time in all the areas that are important to me—taking care of myself, quality time with fam- ily, working, and having fun? Integrity and respect work hand in hand, which we'll delve into in the next chapter, but you can already see how if you respect yourself, you'll take care of your needs. By being in integrity, you're already showing self-respect.

When something comes up you didn't or couldn't plan for, when you are clear on your priorities, it makes it easier to choose what to do in a timely and respectful manner. You don't procrastinate. I remember discussing this in our office one day, and later that week, my daughter, who worked with us at the time, called out to me, "As soon as you know!" in that kind of sarcastic but cute way! I hadn't realized I had been saying out loud, "I'm never going to make it on time to meet with her" and other remarks about the work I had to get done and how was I ever going to complete it and meet with my landscaper on time. I didn't even realize I was sitting there procrastinating about it. Ding, ding, ding, awareness! I was, in essence, choosing not to call my landscaper and to be late without letting her know. It forced me in that moment to make a choice. Call and cancel, let her know I'm running late and see if later works for her, or immediately stop what I was doing at the office and leave so I'd be on time. What was the best choice for me in that moment? Was keeping the commitment most important? Or was staying and finishing my project more important? When you know your priorities, you can align to them more efficiently, consciously choosing instead of reacting without being aware.

Competing Priorities

If you want to succeed, you have to listen to yourself, to your own heart, and you have to have the courage to go your own way. If I had listened to all the sceptics and naysayers I've met along my chosen path, not just that first year but all along the way, you know where I'd be today? Nowhere!

—Robert Mondavi

Often we have competing priorities. If we're not clear on which is more important, we'll react to anything that comes up, especially when it relates to both priorities. Career and family are a great example. What choices are you making with your career that might be sabotaging your family priorities?

Even as I'm writing this chapter, my priorities are tested. The phone rings; I see it's my daughter who is traveling from England, and I haven't talked to her in over a week. Although I have a very short window to write, my priority is family, and to spend some quality time talking with her while she's on her layover on her way home aligns to that priority. The choice is easier to make when we are clear. The quality is better because I can be present rather than worried about my writing time. Of course, to balance it, I have to choose how much time to talk and when to get back to my writing.

As we discovered in Chapter 2, it's helpful to rank-order your priorities, so when it comes time to make a tough choice, you'll have more clarity. It won't always be easy, but at least you'll have something to help guide you to make the right choice for you, and then you can focus on areas that will help you toward your goals.

Sometimes competing priorities happen when we allow others to influence our decisions. Years ago, I had a coaching client, Bruce, who was financially successful with his career as a chief financial officer (CFO) for a Fortune 500 company. He was happy with his wife and two children and where they lived. He just had this uneasiness that he wasn't doing what he was supposed to be doing. After a couple of sessions, Bruce revealed how he had wanted to be a football coach, but his father told him that was nonsense and he had to do something that would guarantee financially security. His father had not realized that perhaps if his son were to fulfill his passion in life, he could be even more financially secure. Furthermore, his father's financial concerns were probably exaggerated by his own experiences and fears.

Because so much time had passed, Bruce had given up entirely on anything related to football coaching. In between working on a few other communication and trust issues he was having at work, we focused on how he could fulfill his desire to coach.

Rather than asking himself whether he could coach football, I had Bruce ask himself *how* he could coach football now. At this point in his life, family ranked higher on his priority list than his passion for football, but it was still important to him. He decided to coach part-time at a local community college. By changing the way he thought about this, he was able to fulfill this passion. Bruce shared with me that he no longer regretted anything—he finally felt he was exactly where he needed to be. He was happy—and even more productive and focused at work now!

It can take courage to follow our dreams, especially when we're not encouraged to or we've been instilled with fear. Integrity is about aligning with who we are and having the courage to live in accord with our passions and priorities. And it may not always be practical to choose a job that fulfills your passion, especially when you have other priorities. Be honest with yourself. If I choose any job just for the money, lie to myself about why, conjure up some excuse, and ignore the truth, that's not being honest with myself. Being in integrity is admitting I need to take this job for the money right now, planning to get back on my path of finding the work I'm intended to do or fulfilling that passion in some other way.

When we align to our truth, we are more confident in ourselves, our decisions, and the results. We have clarity and direction. We are more efficient in the things we do. We decide and act, without wasting time wondering or even regretting after we've made the decision.

Accountability Is an Act of Integrity

Concern yourself more with accepting responsibility than with assigning blame. Let the possibilities inspire you more than the obstacles discourage you.

—Ralph Marston

When my daughter was in seventh grade, she came home one day ripping a teacher apart for her inability to effectively teach. As I sat and listened, she ranted about all the reasons she couldn't learn and therefore her grades were slipping. Even though my natural tendency was to jump in, I purposefully waited until she was finished. Then I asked her, "Well, how will you learn the material then?" With a shocked look on her face and some mumbling about how she didn't have any idea, I could see her starting to catch on. She knew she wasn't off the hook for her slipping grades. When I asked her if she wanted to talk about ideas, like going to the library or getting a tutor, all of a sudden the teacher wasn't so bad. I didn't hear much about it after that, and my daughter's grades began to improve.

Integrity is about taking ownership and personal responsibility to make things happen. Accountability is what happens as an outcome of integrity. The Accountability Ladder (see Figure 3.2) is an awareness tool that helps us see whether we're being reactive and powerless (on the bottom rungs) or proactive and responsible (on the upper rungs). When we feel powerless or victimized by our circumstances, we behave in ways that keep us stuck or motionless. When we behave in accountable, powerful, responsible ways, we are moving—taking action.

It's very difficult to take responsibility for something when you are feeling like a victim or out of control. The only thing we can see when we're in victim mode is that it is someone else's fault, or something happened to me to prevent me from doing anything positive, or maybe I'm so oblivious I don't even know or care. It could be that I'm just not aware at all, and I'm going through life simply reacting to everything.

Waiting and hoping can be a very dangerous spot to be in because the hope might hold us in victim mode. Waiting and hoping is not the same as waiting with patience—as is necessary in some circumstances—it's waiting and hoping for something or someone to change and feeling like there's nothing we can do, while nothing is changing.

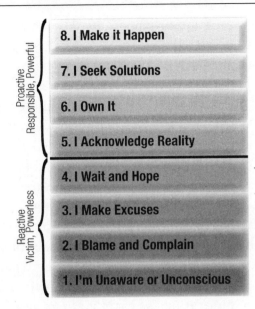

Figure 3.2. The Accountability Ladder
Source: Stewart, J. D. (1984) The role of information in public accountability. Issues in Public Sector Accounting, J.D. Stewart, A. Hopwood and C. Tomkins, Philip Allen, Oxford.

Whenever you are in victim mode, stuck on the bottom rungs, you'll know it by the way you feel. The feeling is usually frustration and stress. Often you'll hear yourself saying things like the following:

"That will never work."

"I tried everything."

"Bad things happen to good people."

"What else could possibly go wrong?"

"It wasn't my fault."

"I should have known better."

"There's nothing I can do."

Paying attention to how we feel and what we say can help us be aware that we are stuck in victim mode. As leaders, parents, and for our own self-improvement, the Accountability Ladder is a great tool to help us see where we are, where we want to be, and how to get there.

A friend of mine owns a restaurant in a very small town. She has had it on the market for many months, while she eagerly waits for the sale! When she took a look at the Accountability Ladder, she realized she was stuck in the wait-and-hope mode. She identified the feeling of frustration immediately and also recognized the words she had been using, such as "there's nothing I can do."

As soon as she acknowledged reality—that it was going to take more than a realtor and a sign to sell the restaurant—she took ownership. She started to think of all the things she could do. For example, she decided to call the realtor regularly to keep her property in the forefront of his mind. She began to provide all appropriate information as soon as it was requested. She proactively thought ahead of what they might need, instead of waiting for the request. She made it her responsibility to communicate with her attorney to make things go faster and more smoothly. This was only the beginning to the solutions she came up with. She's a real go-getter, so she had it in motion, making it happen, almost as we spoke.

There can be a gray area between waiting and hoping and acknowledging reality. Shifting your thoughts to how you can make this happen, not whether you can or can't, will help you get to the upper rungs of making it happen.

It's Not about Being Perfect

The thing that is really hard, and really amazing, is giving up on being perfect and beginning the work of becoming yourself.

—Anna Quindlen

Planning time for the most important things and following through shows integrity. Focus and finish. Do what you say you're going to do. If you say family and health are important to you, do you plan healthy meals or do you skip going to the grocery store when you know you need fresh vegetables? Do you build time in daily or weekly for exercise? Do you make sure you set aside quality time with your family? When the time comes, do you commit or do you reschedule? Often I hear people report that their one-on-ones with their managers are rescheduled so frequently that it feels like it's just not important and actually more of a nuisance to managers than something they want to be doing.

Integrity is not about being perfect, at least not that unattainable definition of perfection that paralyzes many of us. It's about doing your best for yourself, within your means, and staying balanced and happy. As George Orwell said, "The essence of being human is that one does not seek perfection." When you make a mistake or what we'll refer to as a learning experience, you don't beat yourself up over and over again. You look at the truth of it, you accept it rather than deny it, and you move on. It's not that you don't take any responsibility for it. You clean up the mess, but you don't keep dredging it up. So maybe you get frustrated and end up yelling at someone at work. Instead of just leaving it at that, you sincerely apologize and explain your situation. You do your best to not let it happen again. That's integrity.

We're all human, and things happen. When it becomes a pattern of behavior, that's when we need to question ourselves to find out what's up. Do we need to change our behavior or change our priorities? For example, if you're late for a meeting once because something happened that you couldn't avoid, you apologize and take action to get information you may have missed. However, if you're frequently late because you're not planning your time effectively, perhaps you need to figure out your priorities and stay more disciplined. There's usually an underlying thought or belief that is causing you to be late. For example, some people feel they are wasting their time if they arrive too early, so they are frequently late. When you discover why you are late, you can then focus on how to stop being late. In this case, you might bring something to do with you while you wait, so you can be productive.

Perhaps why you're not doing what you say you're going to do is because you are too tired for one or more of your priorities. This is your opportunity to take a good objective look at your choices and actions. Don't beat yourself up over it. There's always something to learn from it. First, go back to your truth and ask yourself if it is really a priority. And if it is, then ask yourself why you're not in integrity. Why are you so tired? What choices are you making that aren't aligning with what you say is important to you? What thoughts might you need to change? What do you need to stop doing, and what do you need to start doing?

As soon as you are aware, you have the opportunity to make a change—perhaps in a thought or a belief or by making another choice in behavior—something that will lead you to feeling good, not regretful. And something that will allow others to trust in you.

Truth + Integrity = Trust

Whoever is careless with the truth in small matters cannot be trusted with important matters.

—Albert Einstein

With truth and integrity comes trust. People experience your authenticity and reliability. They believe you, and they believe in you. You've shown that you can be relied upon. As Stephen Covey says, you've made trust deposits. Trust is critical for leadership, and it creates efficiency and effectiveness in productivity.

In Chapter 2, we talked about how the truth shall set you free. When you are honest, you have nothing to hide. You communicate openly, with fewer reservations. You are less likely to question intentions, you're more willing to forgive and to do so faster, and you'll proactively go the extra mile. Trust creates efficiency.

Reflect for a moment on someone who was a great coach or leader for you. It might have been a past boss or a high school sports coach. Consider what that person did that made such an impact on you. Perhaps it was their belief in you. Maybe it was the way they challenged you to strive to be your best. It could have been the fact that they walked their talk, kept their promises, and followed through. Whatever it was, you can see the power of the impact it made. If that person asked you for a favor, you probably wouldn't hesitate to do it! Great leaders aspire to help others be great and this integrity of their actions creates trust. And trust creates efficiency.

Trust is usually built over time, through a person's consistent actions. We begin to see that what the person says is what they will do. We don't have to second-guess if they will come through; we can rely on them. Knowing what's important (our truth), and living it is what creates trust. We'll learn more about how respect helps us to trust others in Chapter 4. However, we can lose trust much more quickly if we don't align our actions to our words and if we don't focus our intent in the right way.

Why Do People Lie?

Expose yourself to your deepest fear; after that, fear has no power, and the fear of freedom shrinks and vanishes. You are free.

—Jim Morrison

There are all kinds of lies, from exaggerations, to leaving things out, to blatantly lying, and then the little make-life-easier kinds of lies. Those small lies that avoid conflict or make us feel more connected are probably the most common.

A study published in the *Journal of Basic and Applied Psychology* (Levine, Serota, and Shulman, 2002) reported that 60 percent of people had lied at least once during a 10-minute conversation, and several of the subjects lied almost three times during that conversation. Keep in mind that bringing up the topic of lying is not for the purpose of judging it; it's simply to examine it. If we can look at it objectively, we may be able to get past it.

Have you ever thought about why people lie? I've heard all kinds of reasons. They are afraid of being rejected or just not fitting in. It seems that people tend to lie when they're trying to protect their self-esteem. They may also lie because they are afraid of the consequences of their actions. They may be afraid of not living up to someone else's expectations, or they don't want to hurt someone else with the truth.

The basic human need to connect with others can be so strong that we may find ourselves out of integrity, just to try to fit in. Perhaps you overslept, but you find it more acceptable to lie and say that traffic held you up. Your image is protected, and people won't think as badly about you, right?

At times we may even catch ourselves lying to ourselves, denying our own feelings or denying that something just happened. Often we have put ourselves up on this higher self-image pedestal, and we're telling little lies to support that. We are justifying our own deception. We lack the courage to face the truth. What all this lying boils down to is that nasty four-letter F word, fear!

Fear is the culprit. People don't always recognize it as fear; they may think of it as avoidance or something else, but at the most basic level, it is fear.

We're afraid to share our truth. We're afraid to be vulnerable. We don't share our thoughts and dreams with others because we're afraid they will pick on us, just like we don't share our fears with others because we're afraid they'll laugh, or feel sorry for us, or make some other judgment. At some level, we're afraid of being exposed for who we really are and not being accepted.

We're afraid of being judged. So what? What will really happen to you? Will you be ostracized, starved, smothered, stoned, beaten? Thank goodness, we're past those days, but the fear is emotional, and the fear is real, and often people hold on to it without even knowing it.

Take, for example, the fears you might have in performing in public, whether it's speaking, playing an instrument, singing, or playing a sport. When we are nervous, it is difficult to be at our best because we're too busy being afraid of being judged. We may find ourselves lying about why we won't perform in public or making excuses for why we aren't as good as we think we should be. The first step is awareness of our truth. If we're too afraid to perform, perhaps we're looking too much for that connection or acceptance. If we can be honest with ourselves, we can get past our fears.

Have you ever found yourself caught up in complaining or being negative with the group of people you are with? If you think back to your specific situation, you might find you have been partaking in the negativity in an effort to feel connected to them in some way, whether to impress them or just be a part of the conversation. We see it happen in the workplace all the time. Most people may not even be aware that they are doing it. Typically, someone is initiating the conversation and setting the stage for the tone, positive or negative. If this person is the manager, it can be particularly powerful because people feel pressure to follow suit. From there, it is easy to see yourself get caught up in exaggerations or just going along with someone, even though that's not your truth.

Examining our thoughts and beliefs might help us find our truth. When you find it is a fear of something, think about your life and the precious time you have. Think about your freedom of choice to create the life you want. You might find it's better to go after happiness or joy than stay stuck with fear. You might find that the risk is worth it.

Just recognizing the fear begins to tear it down. The mere act of awareness has power in eliminating our fears. (Remember, the truth will set you free.) We've all felt the relief when something is finally exposed or revealed, even when it is negative. It's like a weight has been lifted, and finally there's no need to protect or hide something. At this moment of truth comes choice.

It's hard to escape fear—it is everywhere. Movies are full of fear, deceit, and lies; our media sells fear every day. People find the drama exciting; maybe it stimulates or wakes them up somehow? I think what it's really waking up, though, is the other fears we have within us. Remember, whatever we think about gets played over in our minds 15 to 17 times during the evening, and is nudging the fears in our subconscious brains. It is, in essence, feeding our fears.

There's a story about an old Cherokee teaching his grandson about life. "A fight is going on inside me," he said to the boy.

"It is a terrible fight and it is between two wolves. One is evil—he is anger, envy, sorrow, regret, greed, arrogance, self-pity, guilt, resentment, inferiority, lies, false pride, superiority, and ego." He continued, "The other is good—he is joy, peace, love, hope, serenity, humility, kindness, benevolence, empathy, generosity, truth, compassion, and faith. The same fight is going on inside you—and inside every other person, too."

The grandson thought about it for a minute and then asked his grandfather, "Which wolf will win?"

The old Cherokee simply replied, "The one you feed."

When living in integrity, you accept the truth and your actions around it, and you choose to align to your own truth. It's living authentically, free, full of passion and love, and having a zest for life. It's about having a positive or helpful intent for yourself and those around you.

In a sense, integrity is a prerequisite for respect. We need to be in integrity with ourselves before we can really feel this way about others. If you're angry, jealous, and feeling vengeful, think about your own integrity and truth. What's going on with you? What are you most afraid of?

Before you venture into Chapter 4, take some time to reflect.

What SHIFT Will You Make?

Scan the chapter. List the topics that resonated with you.

_____

_____

Hone in on one or two areas that will make the biggest impact for you.

_____

_____

Imagine the impact. Why is this important? How will you feel when you've accomplished this?

_____

_____

Figure out your plan and how you will stay on track.

_____

_____

Take action. Start now. Schedule it now, and include your follow-up.

_____

_____

Enjoy! Remember to choose to be happy, every step of the way!

_____

_____

References

Levine, T., Serota, K., Shulman, H. (2002). The _Impact of Lie to Me_ on Viewers' Actual Ability to Detect Deception. _Journal of Basic and Applied Psychology_, 37, 847–856.

Nolte, D. (1972). Children Learn What They Live. Retrieved from http://www.empowermentresources.com/info2/childrenlearn-long_version.html.

CHAPTER FOUR

RESPECT—IT'S A TWO-WAY STREET

The respect you show to others (or lack thereof) is an immediate reflection on your self respect.

—Alex Elle

If I have to sit through another one of these meetings, I think I'll explode. Why can't they just run an effective meeting? It's not that hard! Have an agenda, start on time, end on time. Don't get off task. Keep a parking lot for topics that come up that need to be addressed later. And I'm so sick of people not speaking up and then as soon as we leave, the whispers, the complaining. Come on, people! That's why I just couldn't stand it when I could tell that Betty wanted to say something in the meeting, but she refused. It was obvious by her facial expressions. Why couldn't anyone else see this? And now she's mad at me for calling it out. I mean really, I only said,

"I think Betty wants to say something." And for her
to respond with "No, really, I don't" in such a
sarcastic way! With our being the only two women in
the room, I just thought she needed to voice her
opinion. The icing on the cake was her scolding me
afterwards to not ever do that to her again!

R espect is a word we've heard a lot, from our parents telling us
to respect our elders to Aretha Franklin belting out each let-
ter, soulfully demanding respect. Respect is about having admira-
tion for someone; it's about accepting what is without attempting
to change it; it's caring about a thing or a person, having consideration, objectively looking at a person or situation; it's acknowledgment and courtesy. Respect can be both given and received,
and if we don't have self-respect, it's difficult if not impossible
to respect someone else—or to be respected. People will value
and respect you in accordance with the value and respect that
you place upon yourself.

Respect should not be confused with tolerance. Tolerance is
putting up with something or someone. Your energy is more negative and focused on yourself in tolerance. With respect, you are
more focused on the subject, and you feel more positive or at least
neutral. For example, rather than putting up with your employees,
you see them as the vital ingredient for success.

Effective leadership is virtually impossible without respect:
respect for yourself, respect for the people you serve, and respect
for the reality of your situations.

Be Selfish

Respect yourself and others will respect you.

—Confucius

If you cannot respect yourself, it's impossible to truly respect someone else—there will always be doubt and mistrust. To respect yourself, it helps to know your truth and be in integrity. When we respect ourselves and others, we can be more objective about others' behaviors. We can listen to their words without attaching too much significance to them, realizing that they may be motivated by circumstances that have nothing to do with us. We won't think it's all about us. And we won't think we have to jump in and save other people. *Betty can take care of herself!*

Knowing yourself and being true to yourself is the best way to respect yourself. When you're not aligning yourself to your priorities, you are not balanced, and it doesn't feel so good. So when you find you're not balanced or just not respecting yourself in some way, the path is clear—go back to integrity to see where you're not aligning. For example, if you find you keep changing jobs or relationships because you're not feeling fulfilled or happy, go back to examine your truth: What is it that you really want? Is there something preventing you from getting it? At any stage, GRIT® can help us be aware and align. For my client who missed her daughter's dance rehearsal in Chapter 3, she discovered by not saying no to work, she wasn't respecting herself and her priorities. As we learned in Chapter 2, sometimes we can discover this on our own, and sometimes we need help. Respect yourself by getting the support you need.

When we respect ourselves, we can rely on ourselves even more. Take intuition, for example. We learned in Chapter 2 that logic and intuition need to work in harmony. When we are out of balance, it may take the form of paranoia or just not being able to make a decision. When we know ourselves and we stay true to ourselves, we can rely on intuition because we trust ourselves. As Carl Jung said, "Intuition is a function by which you see around corners." We realize our intuition is relying on the information we have gathered and stored along the way.

Growing up, we were taught that being selfish is bad. The message was clear: You should think of others first and not be so selfish! Beliefs and feelings like this can be so powerful they cause us to neglect our own needs. Respecting ourselves first is the only way to be able to authentically respect and give to anyone else. We have to be selfish until we can be generous, meaning we have to take care of ourselves, so we'll have enough to give to others.

Many of us are not in the habit of putting ourselves first. I remember the first time I was on a flight with my 2-year-old daughter. Prior to traveling with her, I really didn't think too much about what the flight attendant was saying. That day I heard clearly what she said, "Put the oxygen mask on yourself before assisting the person sitting next to you." Whoa! Wait a minute—I want to put the mask on my daughter first! But if we don't respect ourselves first, what good will we be to others?

We learned in Chapter 3 that an element of being in integrity includes being whole, being complete, and being balanced. Caring for yourself, your health, your relationships, and anything else that affects your happiness is vital to keeping balanced and whole. Let go of the needless act of suffering, and choose happiness.

Respect expands our focus to considering others. But if we don't keep ourselves balanced and whole, we will end up compromising our own needs, and then it's very difficult to think of others.

Consider Others

You never really understand a person until you consider things from his point of view.

—Harper Lee

Respecting ourselves first doesn't mean we should focus only on ourselves and think it's *all about me*! We need to balance our self-respect with consideration for others. So as we're aligning to our own truth, we have to acknowledge that others are out there with their own truths. Recently on a flight, I watched as one person's priorities and needs interfered with another's. The irritation in her voice interrupted my reading as the woman one row up and across the aisle was loudly complaining to her husband about the smell of feet. I discreetly glanced over and noticed the young man behind her had his shoes off and his socks looked like they'd been worn for months. Maybe he had little consideration for others around him, or perhaps he just had a great need to remove those shoes. I'm sure it was irritating to the woman because she had nowhere to escape the smell. She certainly made it known to all around her the suffering she endured! I don't know if he heard her, and I don't know the reason he had his shoes off. I only know that he never put those shoes back on until we landed.

As important as it is to know ourselves and align to our truth, it is also important that we consider other people and situations. For example, when you or someone you know is trying to make a change, respect the amount of time it might take. I've seen managers request employees to make a change or even put them on a performance improvement plan, and the manager expects change to happen instantaneously. They think just by telling the employees what behavior to change, they'll do it. Even if the employees have changed their thoughts and beliefs around it and are more motivated to do it, it might still take time to change. We are creatures of habit. As Mark Twain said, "Habit is habit and not to be flung out of the window by any man, but coaxed downstairs a step at a time."

Just consider what is happening in our brains as we are creating habits. We focus our attention on what we want to do, and then we repeat it. That repetition is making a little indentation in our brain, and over time it will become ingrained so the behavior is natural; you don't even have to think about it. Yes, creating habits takes practice and patience.

When you have trust in a relationship, you will most likely have some level of respect, but lack of consideration might be more subtle. You could trust a person—say, a teammate—but perhaps not consider that person an equal member of the team. Case in point, a few managers were working on a project together. Two of the managers hadn't been including the third on all the correspondence and, consequently, on an important decision that was made. The two managers claimed they forgot, which they probably did. But why did they forget the third manager? Do they respect that person as a member of the team? Do they feel they are equal parts of the project? They might trust the person but just didn't consider or perhaps value the person enough. I'm sure the third manager had a role in this as well, but we need to consider and respect all angles and views and what we need to make something complete or successful.

So the next time you're making yourself more comfortable or taking care of a priority you have or working on a team—just stop for a moment to consider others you might be impacting. Then make your choice with consideration for your own needs and the needs of others. It might still be more important to you regardless of how it affects others. At least by putting yourself in their shoes, you've considered them; often people don't even give others a thought.

Ego in Disguise

Show respect even to people who don't deserve it; not as a reflection of their character, but as a reflection of yours.

—Dave Willis

A lack of consideration for self or others may be due in part to our ego being out of balance. We're either too focused on ourselves so we're unaware of our surroundings, or we've undervalued ourselves to a point of deprivation. Being overly confident or feeling *more than* can prevent us from considering other people. As Johann Wolfgang von Goethe said, "Being brilliant is no great feat if you respect nothing."

Likewise, minimizing our worth or feeling *less than* can prevent us from considering ourselves. We need a healthy balance of confidence and humility, and respecting our ego for what it is will help us keep it in check.

According to Wikipedia, "The ego separates out what is real. It helps us to organize our thoughts and make sense of them and the world around us." Dictionary.com states it is "the part of the psychic apparatus that experiences and reacts to the outside world and thus mediates between the primitive drives of the id and the demands of the social and physical environment." The ego, simply put, is your expressed self.

Ego can end up disguised as disrespect or some other counterproductive behavior. Most people don't even realize when their ego kicks in to defend them, and people on the receiving end usually perceive it as mean-hearted, condescending, self-centered, and, yes, egotistical! Similar to what motivates us to lie, as we discussed in Chapter 3, the ego is being manipulated by that same four-letter F word—fear!

It may not be an obvious, on-the-surface type of fear; often it's deeper fears that we're not conscious of. These fears put the ego in overdrive. As we discovered in Chapter 2, our emotions can trigger awareness, giving us the opportunity to explore what's driving our actions. Fear is useful, and we shouldn't deny or ignore it. We need to put it in its place—respect it—and be thankful for the awareness. Then we can focus on more productive behaviors.

Take Frank, a very successful partner in an accounting firm who was surprised about his results from his 360 feedback assessment. He told me he actually initiated the 360 process and was looking forward to having his team rate his performance. Both his peers and his direct reports rated him much lower than he rated himself in quite a few areas: creating a motivating environment, coaching, building collaborative teams, communication, and managing performance. He was rated fairly high in results orientation and acting with courage. Many comments indicated that Frank was condescending, not considerate, interrupted, didn't listen, and lost it at times.

After about 25 minutes of defending his behavior and pointing out all his reasons, I dug a little deeper with Frank to find out what he was most worried about and his biggest concerns. It didn't take long to get to why Frank was acting the way he was. He was afraid that everyone else wasn't being productive enough. He was concerned about sales and about setting up the company to be salable for the future. He was stressed out about it and taking it out on everyone around him. He was letting fear (thoughts and beliefs) drive his behavior. Nodding in total appreciation for how he was feeling, I pulled a string out of my bag and laid it on the table. I asked Frank to push the string. As the string bunched up and didn't go anywhere but into a mess, I said, "See what happens when you push people? Now pull the string." As Frank pulled and the string followed along, he hung his head just a little and said, "I've been pushing too hard, haven't I?"

Once Frank was aware, he realized that by allowing his fear to take over and by pushing people, he was making the situation worse. He could now see the importance of changing his behavior. As we know, habits die hard, and Frank wasn't going to change overnight, but the desire was there, which can be half the battle!

You might be thinking, "Wait a minute! Doesn't fear work sometimes?" A healthy dose of fear is what I call respect: having respect for danger, for example, or for our parents. There may be circumstances when fear is necessary, and maybe some of us were so unruly, our parents had to use fear on us when we were younger to keep us safe, but in many situations, it is misused and counterproductive.

As leaders, we have the responsibility to get results through people. Fear may force people to do things, but what do you think they do when you're not looking? And how much energy do you think they put into something, as opposed to how much energy they would put in if they truly respected you?

What Information Are You Filling In?

Assumptions are the termites of relationships.
                                        —Henry Winkler

When people respect you, they want to follow your lead. The goal of a leader is to get a group of individuals to produce results—efficiently, effectively, and enjoyably. It's one thing to focus on ourselves as leaders and be in integrity, showing respect to our own priorities and needs, while being mindful of others' needs. It's another whole challenge to help an entire team do this.

Everyone is different, with unique talents and challenges. Each of us requires different things in order to live in integrity. We can be so self-absorbed in our own priorities that we think everyone thinks and acts just like we do. We assume they are feeling the same way and that their intent is what ours would be. Often we think we undoubtedly know them.

Do you really think you could know someone else? I mean *really* know them? Perhaps your spouse, your child, a best friend, a sibling? Think about it. Did your mom or dad really know you? Everything about you? Your thoughts, your emotions, your fantasies—even your actions? Of course, there's no way for us to really know everything, even if you feel like you're an open book and you share it all! It's hard enough to know ourselves sometimes. So it's easy to see that even if we're good at reading people, it's never a guarantee that we could know what's really going on.

Consequently, we cannot know someone else's intent. We automatically fill in information that isn't there, assuming we know what that person is thinking. When we act as if it's the absolute truth, we end up damaging relationships. It is therefore imperative to communicate clearly, openly, and with respect. In the case earlier, Betty was frustrated in the meeting, but she wasn't willing to speak up. She was making a choice not to, and it wasn't for anyone else to do it for her. When we assume we know what another person needs, we are not showing respect for that person. People's situations and lives are going to be different from ours. There's no way we can know everything about them—or about anything, for that matter.

Think of how many times you thought you knew something was true; you were absolutely convinced of it. And then you found out some new information, and it wasn't at all what you had perceived. There's an old tale about a retired couple who enjoyed their tea every Saturday morning in their cozy little breakfast nook. Like any Saturday morning, the wife was rattling on about this and that, when she noticed her neighbor's laundry was looking a bit dingy. With concern in her voice, she said, "I wonder if everything is all right with Mary. Maybe it's just a detergent she switched to, or perhaps she mixed some colors with the lights. Maybe it's her eyesight." This went on for a few weeks, Mary's condition seemingly getting worse, when one morning as the wife was preparing the tea, she looked up and noticed Mary's laundry was again bright and clean. With great joy, she declared everything was all right with Mary. Her husband responded, "Well, actually, Honey, I washed the windows!" We need to ask ourselves what blinders we are looking through. What do we add to the picture that's not actually there?

Your truth may be different from someone else's truth, just like your perception could be different from someone else's perception. There's so much more to a story than what we see or hear. My grandmother used to say, "Believe nothing of what you hear and only half of what you see." I don't know if I really understood back then, but, wow, does it make sense to me now. For example, it's so easy to get caught up in gossip; we don't stop and even consider if it's the truth. We hear something, and pretty soon we're repeating it, usually embellished for effect or unintentionally leaving out something important! Even when we read things, especially on the Internet, how often do we just believe it without even questioning it?

Human beings have a very intelligent brain, and it's often working all on its own, without any guidance, just putting information together and drawing conclusions. Consider this scenario: It is a rainy night. You drive to the shopping center to pick up some items at the drugstore. You look for a parking place close to the store. The lot is full, but there are two parking places directly in front of the store that are occupied by just one car. The driver of this little sports car has left the car at an angle with part of it in both parking spots. The parking stalls are clearly marked. There is no reason the car could not be parked so that another driver could use the valuable parking space.

Was the driver being considerate of others? What are your feelings when you see something like this? What is your attitude toward the driver?

As Paul Harvey used to say, now consider the rest of the story. You finally park your car. You get to the drugstore and see the driver of the car that is parked in two places run out, jump in the car, and drive away. Once inside the drugstore, you talk to a friend who tells you that there has just been a bad car accident a mile away. The driver of that carelessly parked car that was taking up two parking spaces had driven to the drugstore to get to a telephone to call an ambulance and the police. In his rush to get to a phone, he was most likely not even aware of the way he had parked.

Is there any change in the way you feel now? How about your attitude toward the driver? Whether you think it was right or wrong, or still not a valid excuse to park that way, consider how your mind created a whole drama around it.

It can take patience and discipline to pay attention to what our minds are doing with the information we receive. When we acknowledge that we cannot know the whole truth, our minds shift. Getting in the habit of asking ourselves if there could be any other information or possibilities can alleviate a lot of unnecessary drama. Rather than thinking or saying, "I know," we can replace it with "I wonder." "I know he's chronically late because he just doesn't care" becomes "I wonder if he doesn't care or what is going on."

Respect helps us be free from those lies we identified in Chapter 2, especially our own lies. What information are you filling in that isn't really there? We get very accustomed to drawing conclusions, and we make up lies. Sure, some of us have jobs that require us to make necessary assumptions. But we misuse it—we make assumptions automatically in situations when we really shouldn't. And we believe it's true.

Take empathy for example. When we empathize, we are striving to understand someone else's emotions. We learn to read emotions, but we often jump to other conclusions, such as "Betty wants to say something!" It can be very difficult to not fill in information when you're not receiving any information, especially when you're receiving only nonverbals and you're good at reading and feeling empathy. It makes it seem as if you know the truth. You're sure of it! You're probably completely unaware that you don't have the truth.

Remain Open

People only see what they are prepared to see.
                                        —Ralph Waldo Emerson

When we respect the fact that we don't know someone else's truth, it allows us to consider other options, ask questions, or, at the very least, not act as if we think we have the entire and only truth. It helps us to remain open.

Remaining open and objective to situations is key. Imagine at work if we all were aware of what assumptions we might be making, and rather than acting on them, we simply realize they are thoughts and not necessarily reality. We might ask questions to clarify, we might wait to receive more information, or maybe we just let it go. It all depends on the situation, but we wouldn't jump to conclusions and react negatively.

Although it might be gratifying, it's dangerous when we make assumptions and too often we are right. When this becomes a pattern, it feeds our ego and makes us feel like we're always right. Then we go around touting things like an expert, as if they are truth! We've all known an IKE—the I Know Everything person who irritates us with his knowledge and self-righteousness.

IKE doesn't realize or in some cases doesn't care that there are other views. Someone else may see something differently than you do, and it doesn't mean it's wrong. There are very few things in this world that are absolute truths, and most of those have been argued in one form or fashion, from nature to religion to politics. Truths are typically more relative because most of us are stuck inside our own perceptions. We live our lives according to what we believe is true—that's all we know. Sometimes the difference in views might be a lack of information or perhaps just a different experience. Take wine, as a simple example. Because people have varying taste buds, their preference in wine differs. One is not right or wrong, just different. When you are open to other possibilities and not stuck in the confines of limited thoughts and beliefs, your doors are opened and your horizons expanded.

We all have opinions. We hear them every day. I'm not opposed to opinions; I rather enjoy them. Differing opinions get us thinking. They make life interesting. Creativity and growth can be sparked by conflicting opinions. However, it can be destructive when people present their opinion as the only way, and they don't respect that, first of all, it is an opinion and, second of all, not everyone is going to agree with it. And that's okay. It's a different view; someone sees something differently than you do. If you are confident in yourself, you won't feel the need to defend yourself when someone imposes an opinion on you. You'll be able to say what you want to say, without a lot of drama. You won't feel the need to impose your opinion on the other person.

You'll give others an opportunity to voice their opinions, and you'll respect where they are in their views. And when you do get defensive, well, you know now from reading Chapter 2 that it's an opportunity for awareness, and you can look inside to see what's up with you and discover more about yourself.

Our communication can help show we are open and respectful. When we are present with people, actively listening, empathizing, and acknowledging, they will feel that we are open and that we respect them. On the flip side, if we interrupt, complete their sentences for them, or tune out, we show lack of respect. Realize that people don't know your intent unless you communicate it. All they have is your behavior and your words. Being mindful of our own nonverbals as well as the words we use is important to convey a respectful message. Basic manners and not engaging in gossip are also important. Part II explores communication in more depth.

Respect Other People's Choices

Don't let your luggage define your travels, each life unravels differently.

—Shane Koyczan

There are times when people make choices that you don't agree with. Respect the choices people make. Maybe you don't agree or you feel like that person is just going to get hurt, but why would you think it's for you to rob them of life's experiences?

It's true, there can be a gray area of knowing when to step in and help and when to allow the other person to step up. There are times when you want to help someone avoid what you think is really dangerous or when you just want them to see something they're obviously not considering. Still, enabling someone by doing everything for her, without allowing her to learn and grow on her own, is not respecting that person. We can help someone with awareness and even offer some reasons for different choices, but we still need to allow others to make their own choices and respect the choices they make.

Of course, a pattern of destructive behavior can be an indication that someone needs help. Even then, we need to balance our desires and needs with that of the other person. We have to know where the line is between helping and enabling. How can we help someone see what we see and then leave it up to him if he wants to make a change? If you keep doing it for him, not only will he never learn the lesson but also you'll be resented and blamed on top of it. If Betty made it a habit to send these nonverbal messages and not speak up, then asking her what's up in private might be more effective than blurting it out in front of the entire group. Be aware that your own impatience and frustration may be what inspired you to speak up to begin with, rather than your desire to help.

Accept people as they are. Trying to change other people is not really respecting them, and quite frankly, it might be more about you than about them. When you get the urge to change someone, use that as an opportunity to look at yourself. This happens in romantic relationships all the time. At some point, we start trying to change the other person, who naturally resists. We try harder. The other person resists harder. Do we really respect a person we just want to change?

It doesn't mean that we shouldn't grow, improve, and even influence others. But we need to have realistic expectations. Know our boundaries. Don't try to change things we can't change. My good friend Roseanne Romero always said, "It's like bashing your head against a brick wall. The brick wall's not going anywhere, and you just end up with a big headache."

Accept It, and Let It Go!

Accept—then act. Whatever the present moment contains, accept it as if you had chosen it.... This will miraculously transform your whole life.

—Eckhart Tolle

Integrity taught us to hone in and focus our attention where it's important; respect helps us to stay balanced and not latch on too tightly. Things are constantly changing; time doesn't stand still. Bear in mind the old adage "This, too, shall pass." Because change is constant, we need to learn to not attach too much to something. It's human nature to try to control our environment and hold on to things. When something happens we didn't plan or we can't control, we resist the change—we try to hold on to the old, causing ourselves stress. We need to first accept the new situation and let the old pass by. It's kind of like cleaning out your closet: You've got to let go of some old items to create room for your new treasures.

Accepting something doesn't mean you've been defeated or that you let people walk all over you. Wikipedia defines *acceptance* as "a person's assent to the reality of a situation, recognizing a process or condition (often a negative or uncomfortable situation) without attempting to change it." When it's something you can't change—that brick wall—respect it for what it is, and let it go.

Learning to let go is respecting that we can't control everything. It doesn't mean that we don't care; it means we've accepted it as is. Let it go! Move on! Next! Focus on something you can change. As the saying goes, "Don't sweat the small stuff." Let go of things that aren't really going to matter when you consider the bigger picture.

If you're struggling with letting it go, maybe you need to put some space between you and it. Ever gaze up at the stars on a clear dark night? It's so massive. If you could see the Earth in relation, you'd see how small it is. Yet our Earth seems so huge to us. From a different perspective, you might see how insignificant something is in the grander scheme of things. Or just think from the perspective of the end of your life. When you look back over your entire life, what is really important? What should you let go of? When we put some space between it and us, it helps us put it in perspective, and it helps us let it go.

You might compare it to how you feel sometimes about rain or bad weather. Do you resist it, or do you welcome it? Sure, it's not always what we want for what we have going on, but it is what it is. It's just weather. Nothing personal. No reason to resist it because it will only stress you out. Embrace it. Dress for it. Do what you can with it. But don't go against it. It's not going to change when you resist it, and you're the only one who will end up with a headache or feeling upset and miserable. What good can that possibly do?

And then when you gripe and pass on that negativity to other people, they spread the toxins. You could spread positivity instead, embrace the rain and wind, and be happy regardless. Wouldn't that be refreshing? The weather is no reason to be unhappy. Okay, it's true the sun has vitamin D, and it's probably making us a bit happier. But we don't have to be so miserable when the weather doesn't cooperate. Just think if we could apply that way of thinking to people. We wouldn't be so miserable when they don't cooperate. Treat them like the weather. Let them be. Don't nag about it. Go away for a while and let the storm take its course. Ride it out. Don't try to resist or change people.

So the next time your boss asks you to clean up the break room before those important clients arrive, even though you're frustrated because you always clean up after yourself and everyone else leaves it a mess, don't resist doing it or try to change the situation. Act as if you want to clean it up! Do it, and move on!

If someone takes credit for something you did or doesn't thank you for something, even though it irks you beyond measure, pretend you want it that way. Let it go. Move on!

Our ego doesn't take rejection well. When that special friend doesn't call or someone close to you doesn't do what you expect, it's hard not to feel emotional about it. Remember, it is what it is. Whether your situation seems petty or paramount, if it's something you can't control, let it go. Move on! Get over it! Next! Find the phrase that motivates you to let it go.

There's nothing you can really do to change other people, so why would you want to suffer with the way you feel about what they are doing? Why would you bash your head against that brick wall?

Believe in Your People

When nobody around you seems to measure up, it's time to check your yardstick.

—Bill Lemley

Many of us know that jobs and relationships can be unbearable when we don't feel valued and respected. For example, while I was working with Jeremy, a promising sales executive on a fast development track, he complained of his sales manager "riding his ass and not respecting him." This was verbatim multiple times from Jeremy. He tried talking to his boss, but "it went nowhere." In fact, in Jeremy's view, it had backfired. His boss was even more sarcastic afterwards. Jeremy definitely wanted to work hard and earn a good living, but not at the expense of his personal life. It was important to him to keep his personal and work lives separate. Felix, his sales manager, worked all hours and combined his personal and work time. He thrived that way and expected Jeremy to be the same way. Jeremy was resentful and felt disrespected.

Perhaps this culture wasn't a good fit for Jeremy, but it didn't help that neither of them was being clear on their expectations or respecting different priorities and work styles. They hid behind sarcasm and avoidance, and the problem festered. When Jeremy left, Felix declared that Jeremy's heart was just not in it, while Jeremy left only because of the disrespect he felt from Felix.

As a leader, how do we earn the respect of our people? It starts by believing in our people—being able to visualize their success and trusting in their potential to achieve great results. We do this by considering each one as a unique individual and adapting accordingly, by genuinely caring for each person as a human being, and by treating each person as a vital asset to your organization. It's the same with our personal relationships. We need to treat our parents, our siblings, our children, our spouse, our friends, and anyone else in our lives as unique and important individuals, with diverse needs and varying ways of communicating. When we truly appreciate other people as equals in our relationships, we earn their respect.

Similar to parenting, a really good manager will be inconsistent with his approach and interaction with people, giving each one what they need, not just what is comfortable to the manager. For anyone who has children, you've learned you have to parent each one uniquely, and so it is with leading people. Case in point, sarcasm may have worked with some individuals, but Felix's sarcasm was ineffective with Jeremy. Furthermore, if a manager is appreciative of DiSC® styles, she will adapt to more effectively communicate and relate to her team. Focusing on the benefit of uniqueness and respecting the needs of others inspires creativity and fosters loyalty.

Caring for each individual on your team, as a human being, shows a tremendous amount of respect. When you can show that you relate and empathize with a person's situation, it goes a long way. As we know, it's not about being perfect, so share your vulnerabilities. Sharing shows that you are real and not up on a pedestal of untouchable perfection. And it will show that you can relate to others' situation. It doesn't mean you enable them or ignore important behaviors that might need to change. You can show you get it and move on to helping them realize what needs to change.

You will also earn respect if you are helping to influence someone's growth and development. People feel appreciated when you take a genuine interest in them. On the other hand, if you are micromanaging every detail and overly concerned with a person's every move rather than focused on the overall results, you're on a fast track to being disrespected. Micromanaging sends the message that you don't trust the person. Obviously, if the results are lacking, performance needs to be addressed. If you broach the situation with respect—for example, by asking the person how you can help them achieve the results—you help build respect.

Walking the talk earns respect. Actions speak louder than words. Telling others what to do, but not doing it yourself, sets the stage for disrespect. Arrive to your meetings on time. Make phone calls punctually. People are more likely to respect you if you do the things you say you'll do at the times you say you'll do them.

We earn respect with our teams if we encourage conflict and healthy debate, first by demonstrating the behavior ourselves. When we avoid important issues that need to be discussed or we neglect to follow through on a sensitive subject, we end up losing people's respect. Empowering the team to communicate openly shows you have respect for each member's ability to handle these situations, without the need to step in.

A manager who interferes with personal time by e-mailing people at all hours of the evening and weekend can cause angst, especially if the manager has preached the opposite. Even if people aren't expected to reply, they feel the pressure to do so. And if there are other subtle hints that employees should be attentive and working during their personal time, it all adds up to stress and resentment. You will earn more respect by being clear on what you expect. Most employees will not tell their boss how they are feeling, but their productivity is definitely impacted, and it's dangerous because you may never be able to trace the negative repercussions.

Even as teammates or family members, if we're not considering other people's time, we're sending a message of disrespect. Typically, it's not intentional; most of us aren't even aware that we're not thinking of the other person's time. For example, we interrupt because something popped into our head, but really we could wait our turn or even talk about it at a scheduled time. Respect for other people's time just takes awareness and consideration, and it also helps you to earn their respect.

You Can't Demand Respect

You can't build a relationship with a hammer.
—Unknown

Respect is not something we can demand. We can't make someone respect us. Just think about it: Can someone make you respect them? You might obey them or put up with them, but do you really respect them, unless you want to? We earn respect through our actions.

If you're constantly looking for respect, it may be time to hold up that mirror. Are you showing respect to others? Are you respecting yourself? Generally, what we are searching for can be exactly what we need to be giving. Once we start giving respect, we'll start receiving respect.

We can't demand respect, or forgiveness, for that matter. It doesn't work that way. Forgiveness can be seen as an extension of respect. If you respect yourself—if you value yourself—you will allow yourself forgiveness. Start by respecting and forgiving yourself first. It's important to understand that, technically, you can't really hurt someone else because you're not in control of their feelings. That does not, however, give people a license to be mean and do hurtful things, like purposefully lying or taking advantage of someone. People who are mean or do hurtful things are out of integrity by not aligning their behaviors to their truth. When we receive negative behavior, it is the responsibility of each one of us to do our best to stay aligned to our own truth, respect ourselves, and not put up with other people's abuse.

This doesn't mean we won't have feelings and express them, and it doesn't mean we should reject or deny other people's feelings. However, most of us put ourselves through more negative emotions than necessary. And then we feed off the drama. All we're talking about here is committing to taking care of ourselves, so we can best deal with life's upsets.

At the same time, realize that if you do wrong someone else, they very well may forgive you, and hopefully they do. But that does not mean they are obligated to keep you in their lives. Respect the fact that forgiveness and respect are that person's choice—you can't demand them.

Of course, sometimes respect or forgiveness should be given, and it's not. If children aren't raised to respect others or to respect their things, they may not even know how to respect or forgive, and they may not understand the value of it. They won't have consideration for other people, and they won't take care of things. They will most likely have lower self-esteem, and it will be masked in some way. These people who didn't learn to respect may be the ones you'll want to demand respect from. Although we can't demand it, we may be able to teach it. We may be able to earn it. But we need to respect that this is where they are, and they may need to experience a bump in their road.

Bumps in the Road

Success and failure are on the same path; success is just a little further down the road.

—Cathy Collaut

It's inevitable that we will experience setbacks, failures, big mistakes, learning experiences—call them whatever you want. Remember, we're not perfect in that unattainable perfection way, and these mistakes can be some of life's best opportunities for awareness.

Unless we're sitting home on the couch watching TV all day and not out living life and exposing ourselves to risk, we will trip up at times. (Quite frankly, I think sitting on the couch would be one of the worst mistakes.) If you're not tripping up, you're not taking enough chances. When we do trip up, we've got to learn to get back on track; just think of it as if there's no other choice. It's a must. When we have goals, priorities, values, dreams, there will be bumps in the road. It takes courage and tenacity to keep going. Intentional leaders know how to deal with setbacks, and they help others deal, too—in a respectful manner.

So first, we have to accept mistakes as inevitable. It's not a matter of will it or won't it. It will happen. To get to success, we will make mistakes on the way.

When you do make a mistake, once you accept your mishap, give yourself a little time to grieve if you need to. It's a form of loss when you don't meet your own expectations. Respect your need to put closure to it. Just don't stay there. Remember, this too shall pass, and move on as soon as you're ready. Put it in perspective: Recall the vastness of the stars on that dark night mentioned earlier, and think of it as just one of those tiny lights. Put some space between you and it. It does not define who you are; it is just one little experience you had, and you're making it bigger than it needs to be. Let it go.

Respect yourself for the effort you put in. Be cognizant that there are many potential outcomes, and you don't have control over everything. There could be a dozen other factors that contributed to the so-called failure. Lighten up about it. There are many more chances to take! Move on, with a feeling of gratitude. Be thankful for the experience and opportunity to live your life and take chances. If you're finding a pattern of similar mistakes, take the time to explore what might be just a little bigger bump in the road.

Respect Your Journey

Sometimes it's the journey that teaches you a lot about your destination.

—Drake

Respect that we have been conditioned and shaped our entire lives. Perhaps you are now just waking up, or maybe you've been at this awareness stuff for a while. Wherever you are on your path of awareness, it helps to have an appreciation of the process. Patterns and habits in our thoughts, emotions, and behaviors have been created over many years. Some of them may be very hard to remove because they are set in like fossils in a stone. Emotions make it tricky because our emotions have memory. At times, we experience an event, and we get emotional without even knowing why. We have past memories that we've suppressed or locked away, and we don't even realize it. Then when we experience something today that triggers that emotion, we don't realize why. We might be fearful or anxious or sad. Stop. Reflect. Analyze your feelings and emotions before moving forward. Is it a past issue? Respect your emotional memory. Just bringing awareness to it will help dissipate it.

With awareness and respect for your truth and an appreciation of the path you are on, you will enjoy yourself the entire time, rather than only looking forward to your destination. You will feel accomplished every step of the way.

Before you venture into Chapter 5, take some time to reflect.

What SHIFT Will You Make?

Scan the chapter. List the topics that resonated with you.

_____

_____

Hone in on one or two areas that will make the biggest impact
for you.

_____

_____

Imagine the impact. Why is this important? How will you feel when you've accomplished this?

_____

_____

Figure out your plan and how you will stay on track.

_____

_____

Take action. Start now. Schedule it now, and include your follow-up.

_____

_____

Enjoy! Remember to choose to be happy, every step of the way!

_____

_____

CHAPTER FIVE

GENEROSITY—THE MORE YOU GIVE, THE MORE YOU GET

When you give you always get more back in return. I'm not talking about material terms; I'm talking about a return in satisfaction and joy. Generosity pays.

—Robert Mondavi

There's just not enough time in a day. I've got way too much to do and not nearly enough time to complete it all. The time it takes to manage this team and workload is insane. There's certainly not enough time for quality meetings with direct reports. And I'm supposed to give feedback, too? When do I fit that in? I'm feeling so rushed I can't even hear when someone is telling me something. My mind is on a dozen other details.

> Even at home it feels like I can't get up early
> enough. There's never time for exercise, let alone a
> nice breakfast with the kids before we all rush off.
> I don't know where the evenings go, except getting
> supper on, cleaning up, and finishing up project tasks
> for the next day at work. Something's got to give!

Can you imagine if you genuinely felt like you had plenty of time: plenty of time to do the things you wanted to do, plenty of time to listen fully to your child, plenty of time to help your coworker, plenty of time to hear what is being said? How would it feel to not be rushed, overwhelmed, stressed out; to actually feel happy and productive on a consistent basis?

When you are living in integrity with your truth, and you respect yourself and others, you will naturally feel generous; it's not forced. You'll have aligned yourself properly, so your generosity is channeled in a way that makes sense for you. You have enough to go around. You've charged your own battery, you're happy, and you care about others. You feel like you have enough time, you have enough patience, you have enough energy—you simply have enough! In a sense, generosity is the reward for the work put in with truth, integrity, and respect.

In Chapters 3 and 4, we talked about the element of being in integrity that includes being whole, being complete, and being balanced. Caring for yourself—health, relationships, and anything else that affects your happiness—is vital to keeping balanced and whole, so when you are giving, you are giving your best.

According to Dictionary.com, generosity is largeness or fullness; it is amplitude. It is also defined as "readiness or liberality in giving." When a person isn't happy or fulfilled in some way, it can be more difficult to be generous in a healthy manner. When we are complete, healthy, and whole, we can give authentically without feeling depleted.

Pay It Forward

Let no one ever come to you without leaving better and happier.

—Mother Teresa

There is another definition of *generosity* that means "freedom from meanness or smallness of mind or character." In other words, as mentioned in past chapters, our intent is in the right place. We are giving out of genuine caring or love. We don't have ulterior motives or hidden agendas. Not only are we on this earth to find happiness but also we're here to extend it to others. The generosity meter becomes a great mirror. If you are truly happy, you will genuinely want others to be happy.

Wikipedia states: "Generosity is the habit of giving without expecting anything in return. It can involve offering time, assets or talents to aid someone in need. Often equated with charity as a virtue, generosity is widely accepted in society as a desirable trait." It's the pay it forward concept. If you haven't seen the movie, it's worth watching. The concept is to give to someone—with your time or talents, perhaps money if that's what you have plenty of—without expecting anything in return. In the movie, the boy Trevor has to come up with a social studies project, something that will change the world, and he is tasked to put it into action. Trevor comes up with the idea of paying a favor not back, but to pay it forward and keep the generosity moving forward with three good deeds done to three new people. The act of giving anonymously is a way to guarantee not getting anything in return, and as seen in the movie, it can be very rewarding emotionally.

I've shared this story in my classes over the years, and I've heard many incredible examples of what people have done in the spirit of pay it forward, from cleaning off people's snow- and ice-covered cars, to paying for their tolls on the expressway.

It doesn't have to be money; it's just an act of giving that creates happiness for another person. It's thinking about making someone else's day. If you haven't tried giving anonymously yet, check it out. Mail someone a $20 bill with no return address. Or leave it somewhere you know they'll get it. Mow someone's lawn. Pay for someone's meal behind you in the drive-through line. Pay for some tolls or coffees. Shovel someone's sidewalk. Just look for something you can do to give anonymously. It doesn't always have to be anonymous, but it's a good practice to see how it feels to not need the recognition. There's nothing wrong with receiving a thank you, but anonymity takes away the expectation of giving something back. The feeling is really cool, almost liberating.

When you give anonymously, there's a quiet happiness and peace inside. When you start to make a habit of this, it helps you to stop needing the acknowledgment and recognition. You begin to understand your own needs. Many of us want to be acknowledged when we give, and we expect something back—at the very least, a thank-you. When we depend on the recognition, it becomes a negative, needy energy. We can still appreciate it when someone wants to acknowledge or recognize us, but we don't need to rely on it.

How do you know when you're expecting something in return or even depending on it? Think for a moment about how you feel if you don't get acknowledged for being the source of that funny joke or valuable information, especially if someone else is getting all the credit. Do you get upset if you don't get a thank-you card from a wedding or shower you attended and generously gifted? A client was recently talking about how rude it was that the organization never received acknowledgment for a large donation. Of course, it's good manners to thank and acknowledge others, but the point here is to be aware of how much you depend on it.

When you're giving anonymously, remember that it is also good for a person to receive something with no possible way of giving back. Sure, it might drive some people crazy trying to figure out where the gift came from, but they will still feel the pure generosity at some level. It also provides that person with the opportunity to practice pure gratitude.

It has been scientifically proven that the regular practice of gratitude can dramatically change your body's chemistry, giving way to a more peaceful body and mind. The HeartMath Institute has 15 years of scientific research proving that a simple tool like the art of gratitude can dramatically reduce stress and improve performance for individuals and organizations (Institute of HeartMath, 2014).

Many Fortune 500 companies are now starting to use gratitude techniques to reduce work-related stress. Countless books have been written on the subject, including *Simple Abundance* by Sarah Ban Breathnach (2009) and *The Thank You Book* by Robyn Freedman Spizman (2002). Gratitude journals are available, and talk show hosts like Oprah are encouraging nightly gratitude rituals.

While we know it's healthier to not depend on recognition, it is a reality that many of us still need it. We might need it to heal ourselves, to build our confidence, to become complete, so we can give to others. It's good positive energy when we give thanks and recognition. So while we're working on not needing it, go ahead and continue to give it. Give it in an authentic way, without expecting anything back. Give it out of pure appreciation and gratitude. Give with joy, with happiness—not because you have to or because you expect something in return.

The paradox is that you get more when you give more. But your intent can't be only to get more because the energy around it will repel, and you won't get more. When you give authentically, there is a different spirit around it. As soon as you let go of the need to get back, that's when you'll get back. When you least expect it. Not in the way you thought you would because, again, letting go of the expectation was a necessity to make it happen.

Let It Flow

Abundance is not something we acquire. It is something we tune into.

—Wayne Dyer

Perhaps you're very generous, but you find it difficult to accept generosity from others. Deepak Chopra in *The Seven Spiritual Laws of Success* (Chopra, 1994) teaches us about the law of giving (and receiving). It's not just about giving; it's about receiving as well, in order to keep the flow going. If you can't receive, you are stopping the flow of someone giving.

Being able to accept someone else's generosity is as important as being generous to others. Do you allow others to help you or give to you? How do you feel when someone gives you a gift? Do you instantly feel bad because you didn't get them a gift? Or maybe you're contemplating how to even up and get her a gift. When we aren't accepting generosity gracefully, we can go back and look at our truth, integrity, and respect.

Take the flow of money and the effect of giving and receiving. The word *affluence* has its root meaning in *flow*, as does the word *currency*. Money is meant to be exchanged for services and goods. If we hoard it, the flow stops. If we can't receive it, the flow stops.

When we do engage in the exchange of money, through giving and receiving, we keep the flow going, and it comes back. It's a healthy spirit of giving that doesn't deplete your own resources but actually enhances you.

Have you ever noticed that when you're feeling confident and truly happy with yourself, you naturally give more? You want to give; you don't feel like you have to give. It's a feeling of abundance rather than scarcity. When we're feeling scarce, we feel the need to be greedy, to hold on to things and not give them away. We're afraid there's not enough. We're protecting ourselves in some way. Many of us have been taught to believe in a limited supply. I can remember my grandmother, probably because she grew up in the depression, obsessing over saving electricity and material items to the extent of washing the wax paper from the cereal boxes and using it over. We use to joke with her about reusing her toilet paper!

Generosity is an expression of love and abundance. Greed is an expression of fear and scarcity. When we are greedy, we worry that there's not enough of something, or we take more than we need of something because it fulfills some other unmet need. Take money, for example. If we're constantly feeling like there's not enough, we certainly won't feel like we can give any away. And that energy around the feeling of scarcity will repel the kinds of things you might need in your life to create more money. No matter how much money you have, feel grateful for it, and the energy will transform from scarcity to abundance.

There are many examples from history of how greed has caused destruction. Take the sad story of how the buffalo nation was destroyed a century ago in North America. "The Indian was frugal in the midst of plenty," says Luther Standing Bear, a member of the Lakota tribe. "When the buffalo roamed the plains in multitudes, he slaughtered only what he could eat and these he used to the hair and bones." On a recent client visit in British Columbia, I was reminded of this when on a wine tour with a local manager. He was sharing how they used noise to keep the deer and bear away from the vineyards. We got into a discussion about hunting and how it has become more of a sport, rather than a respectful practice for food, clothing, and other uses. Many hunters today are out there only to feed their egos; they just want the recognition of the biggest or best kill. Abundance is not about being wasteful; greed can often result in waste and deprivation.

Another classic example of scarcity is the feeling that there's not enough time. It's epidemic in our society. We put way too many things in a day, a week, a year. We try to cram so much in that we aren't even enjoying a large majority of our time.

Parents think they have to fill their children's schedules to make sure they are getting everything they possibly can to be as competitive as they can possibly be. Parents believe their children need all these skills, volunteering experience, involvement in community, sports, and arts to get into the best college and get the best job and make the most money and have the most things. It's exhausting!

Add to that the vast amount of choices made very accessible by media and the Internet, and we start to feel we need what that other person is having or experiencing. We lose touch of what's most important to us and get caught up in the next best thing. It's true that it can be difficult with all of this in front of us. It takes even more mindfulness to make careful choices, when ironically mindfulness is what we have the least of. It's a cyclical never-ending problem—unless we commit to being aware and making better choices.

Think about it: If you're clear about what you want and you're living your life in alignment with that, respecting yourself and others, you will have plenty of time to do the things that are most important to you. Perhaps you're trying to do too much or you have too much? If that resonates with you, if you're finding some truth in that, simply ask yourself why. Self-reflect to figure out what might be driving your behavior. Have you lost touch with your priorities? Are you getting caught up with the Joneses, trying to keep up with your neighbors or coworkers? Do you have the fear of not having enough or of not being good enough without all the material trappings?

Overly Generous

Life is funny. Things change, people change, but you will always be you, so stay true to yourself and never sacrifice who you are for anyone.

—Zayn Malik

Is there really such a thing as being overly generous? Certainly, if you are not respecting yourself or perhaps not respecting another individual, you may be too generous. It's only too generous if there is a negative outcome for you or the recipient.

Generosity is such a desirable trait in our society that people can end up giving at the expense of themselves or others. We are often told to give to others and that will bring us joy. Will it really if we don't respect ourselves and stay true to ourselves? Might we feel resentful? Perhaps we'll give too much and deplete ourselves. We may even find ourselves addicted to the feeling we get when someone needs us.

We all know someone who gives the shirt off his back but then ends up freezing and ironically becomes a burden. When you deprive yourself, you're not really doing anything helpful in the long run. You're not staying true to yourself, and the generosity you think you're giving is actually draining another person.

While generosity can sometimes be very healing for a person, it becomes a problem when you give to others to make yourself feel good and you become addicted to the feeling of being needed. Because there's such pressure from society to be generous, you might find yourself faking it to look good or fit in. Typically, this person finds it difficult to receive from others and feels resentful or depleted because of it. For example, during arguments, if you are overaccommodating, you might end up later feeling self-pity and resentment. Another example of trying to fit in or look good is the people who volunteer because they're supposed to, not because they authentically want to. Some people give at church because it's the thing to do, not because it's from their heart.

You give so much perhaps because you have an unfulfilled need to be wanted, to be loved, to be important, to be connected. You want so badly to be connected to a group, a person, or a cause that you do everything for that person, group, or cause, hoping that they just can't live without you. You give and give and give, you don't get anything back, and it feels like people take advantage of you.

Some people participate in romantic relationships this way. They give so much because they feel they must to get loved back. They give way too much, and they do it because subconsciously they want to be loved, but it backfires because it's too much. The energy behind it is desperate or smothering, and it pushes the other person away. Anything in life is like this. If we go over the line and do too much, it causes a different energy that's actually repelling rather than attracting.

Often the people who are overly generous are expecting something in return. Whether it's an emotional need, like feeling appreciated, or it's something tangible, like a gift, they are looking for something. But they don't come out and ask for it, and they wind up feeling resentful when they don't get it. It's not healthy for anyone.

Whether it's a romantic relationship or a professional relationship, if we respect ourselves and others, we will ask for what we want. And if we don't get it, we won't stick around someone who's not loving and appreciative. Rather than get yourself in a funk and be upset about not getting what you expect from a person, move on. It's hard, yes, because we've become attached to that person or attached to the feeling we get from them. When we feel this attachment, it's a great opportunity to look inside and find out why. Maybe you need to be more generous to yourself. Go back and see what's really important to you (your truth). Are you aligning your thoughts, beliefs, and activities to your truth? Perhaps you're not respecting where this other person is right now on their life path.

When you give too much, you can also end up depriving the other person. You may end up enabling someone rather than allowing that person the opportunity for a learning experience. You pick them up every single time they fall, and you clean up all their messes. What does this teach them? You could be robbing them of some of life's greatest experiences. And if you take a good hard look, it's more about some need you're looking to fulfill—to be needed, to feel like a hero, to get attention?

We talked about respecting other people's choices and the paths they are on in Chapter 4. When we give too much, we can ask ourselves why we don't respect these people enough to let them live their lives. Sure, if it's something very dangerous, we may need to step in. Those times are rare. You'll know you're disrespecting people if you constantly think they need to be saved: They can't pick the right job, the right guy, the right whatever. You might want to ask yourself, Do I not trust this person to figure out life?

Case in point, when parenting, it may seem like the pendulum may have swung too far. We tend to overcompensate for our lack with our kids today. Perhaps we felt deprived in our childhood, or we are feeling guilty for not spending enough time with them, or we think to survive in this world they need us, so we step in and fix everything for them. It seems we've created a sense of entitlement with a touch of self-centeredness by being too generous.

There are also people who seem to not give enough or only give when there is a benefit to them. Did you ever notice that when certain people call, you feel, "What do they want now?" There's probably a pattern with them that they call only when they need something. Because they don't just call or contact us from time to time to say hello, without needing anything, we become resentful or just irritated about it.

GRIT® helps us be clear on what's important to us, to not judge others and make assumptions about their motives. We take care of our needs, and we don't overcommit to make someone else happy. We give to them if we can and if we want to, not because we feel like we should or we have to. And we don't resent that we gave of ourselves.

It is about balancing your needs and taking care of those first, so you can then be generous with others. So yes, it is about being generous with yourself. If you keep your body healthy, you'll have the energy and drive to do things. If you keep your soul and your mind happy, you'll have the energy and drive to give to others.

Comparable to when you're sick and you don't have the energy to do what you'd like to, when you're not feeling good about yourself, you don't have enough to give to others. So if you're not feeling generous, or maybe you're giving too much and depleting yourself, look inside to discover what's going on. Are you respecting yourself? Have you aligned your priorities?

Being overly generous is simply another opportunity for us to take a good look in the mirror. When you're only happy giving to others, and you either feel guilty or get no satisfaction from giving to yourself, then that's a sign you might be overly generous in an unhealthy way. It's really important that we give in a healthy way because positive energy will be passed along with the giving.

Finding Purpose

We rise by lifting others.

—Robert Ingersoll

Sometimes thinking of what you can give to others, what gift you have, can help you find purpose and meaning in your life. When we feel like we're doing something important that makes a difference, it helps us feel connected—in a healthy way. What can we give to the world that we're passionate about, that we're good at doing, and that can make us a decent living? Sometimes being generous can be the way to find your truth. So we don't always start with truth. We sometimes start elsewhere in GRIT®. Once we find that purpose, we align to it and go through the GRIT® road map. While GRIT® helps us stay aligned, and happy, it can also help us get back on track when we feel lost and without purpose.

Recently I was talking with a retired woman who had lost her husband and whose children were now grown and had moved away. Because her whole identity had been her family and partially her prior work, she was feeling she had no purpose. She was depressed. She was looking back at her life, constantly wishing for what she had in the past. She couldn't afford to visit family often enough, and even when she did, she said she frequently felt out of sorts, longing to go home but then missing them as soon as she was back home.

As we were talking, she became aware that she had lost her purpose and felt like she was aimlessly drifting. She wanted to feel connected and give back to society. Without work and family, she felt this avenue had closed. She started to think about all the things she could do that maybe others could appreciate, while she could feel connected and make some small contribution. I intentionally talked with her more about it, so she would realize that there will be some trial and error. Maybe she wouldn't find the right thing right away. Perhaps she would need to try things out and see what inspired her. She agreed she needed to be patient through it. (Remember patience means waiting and being happy!)

In her past, she didn't have to try; it seemed like things just fell in place. Looking for something meaningful seemed strange and foreign to her, and she realized she had beliefs that she shouldn't have to force something, that it should just flow easily. We talked about it more, helping her to see that it really wasn't forcing anything, but rather opening up and experiencing life. Perhaps she had shut down along the way.

With those words, she had a physical reaction. She realized she had closed up. She didn't know how or when, but she knew it was the truth. She also realized then that she could open back up and that she could indeed control this. It was not just happening to her. It was a very empowering moment for her. She felt like a weight was lifted. We talked about the many things that she could give, and she decided she'd try one, volunteering at the local children's cancer center, and she'd also take up something just for her own pleasure, a quilting circle.

We talked about the importance of giving to yourself as well as to others, so you don't feel this empty void when family is gone, when you retire, or during any other transition in your life. Learning to live happily with yourself first creates a much healthier love and connection with others, and then you won't be so sad and depressed through those transitions. We can start at generosity. Start by giving, and this will open your heart. But make sure you balance generosity, so you are not depleting yourself or others.

Generosity at Work

We make a living by what we get, we make a life by what we give.

—Winston Churchill

Generosity will extend to all areas of your life, including work. When you're authentic, your thoughts and behaviors and words come from a place of good intent. There's no reason to sabotage, feel greedy, lie, or cheat. When we respect ourselves, our intent is helpful, not harmful. We feel abundance rather than scarcity. Generosity comes naturally. We become more focused on helping others, whether it's a manager developing her direct reports, a salesperson helping his prospect with a solution, or a team member committed to the project.

It's the same across all industries; workplaces are being required to produce more with less. This sense of scarcity is causing people to feel they don't have enough time. For example, we may feel we can't even pick up that piece of trash or rinse the coffee pot because we don't have time. In reality, we do. Just with the time we spent thinking about it, we could have done it. But we feel overwhelmed and resist because of the pressure of not enough time. Our thoughts and beliefs about the scarcity of time influence our actions. And in this case, it's causing us to have less time then we actually do. We feel we don't want to take the time to do it because we're just too tired mentally or physically or our attitude is stuck in resistance mode.

Rather than feeling completely overwhelmed, by practicing GRIT® you not only get things accomplished but also have the energy to have fun and find humor in things. The not-my-job mentality goes away. Instead of work, it feels like play! It's effortless and very enjoyable. And yes, it's much more efficient and productive!

We listen more fully and are more engaged. Relationships improve, ideas flow, and productivity increases. We know where to focus our attention. It doesn't take as much energy to be disciplined and develop habits. You don't feel forced. Authentic generosity is giving because you want to, not because you have to.

As a manager, you'll be eager to give that tough feedback because your intent is to help. This will trickle down to teammates, and they will want to help each other stay on track. Giving feedback is an opportunity for awareness, and you respect that those receiving it can decide if it's true for them and if they need to adjust to be in integrity with themselves. You'll naturally acknowledge people for the efforts they put in because you know it helps them stay on track and keep motivated. We'll dive deeper into feedback in Chapter 11.

Just imagine, turf wars diminish because people are providing more information to each other. Fear dissipates. Our egos no longer need to protect us. We have a genuine desire to help by providing the appropriate information and sharing tools. Other people and departments experience the positive results, so they reciprocate. Of course not everyone is going to automatically trust and be open with everything just because you have begun to. We need to respect that some wounds are deeper than others and take more time to heal. Bear in mind we don't have to expect anything in return. When we give information to the other department or person, give it without the expectation of being paid back. Remember, pay it forward. Eventually it will come back. It's the law of nature.

A workplace where everyone practices GRIT® is a productive and enjoyable place that embraces and drives change! People are there because they want to be, not because they have to be. There's a feeling of ownership that naturally has people holding themselves and each other accountable. The positive energy inspires creativity. GRIT® builds character and tenacity, so people are tough enough to see things through, to stick it out, and to endure when times are tough.

And Now, the Rest of the Story

It was difficult at first to admit that it was me creating or at least allowing the chaos. Feeling overwhelmed at work, at home, and quite frankly in all areas of my life was one clue that I may be the common denominator. Yup, I had it bad—the White Knight Syndrome! My ego needed it. Taking on all that work, staying late at the office, and not getting enough sleep made me feel worthy, special, connected. When people were feeling sorry for me, it fed the need I had. It wasn't healthy. The good news was that I was doing it to myself. Why is that good news? Because I could undo it, too!

By being completely honest with myself, starting with my truth, I began to make changes in my life. For example, looking at my actions and thoughts and beliefs, I could see this was the unhealthy White Knight syndrome, rather than a healthy generosity, genuinely helping someone else. Being aware of my intent is what cut right to it. Asking myself "Why am I doing this? What am I feeling?" helped bring clarity. As we've discussed, emotions can be a great way to identify our real intent. Sometimes we have to dig a little deeper than the surface, because it can be easy to fool ourselves. Feeling like a victim and feeling a need for other people to think of me as a busy important person were some pretty good warning signs.

Since I've been practicing GRIT®, I've noticed how I feel different. I'm not looking for approval or pity from others. I work shorter hours and get more done—and make more money. I feel satisfied and content with where I am in my life, yet I am still eager to learn and grow. I'm not always looking toward the future for my happiness; I choose happiness in the now. When I get off-track, I notice pretty quickly and take responsibility to get myself aligned.

When you have true, authentic generosity, it comes back to you in a thousand ways. It's like having your cake and eating it, too! It's just the way it works. The combination of GRIT® creates this in our lives, be it on the job, at home, or in our social lives. The reward comes in passion for what you do, energy to fulfill your dreams, and other acts of authentic generosity.

When we practice GRIT®, we suffer a lot less. We can be aware much more quickly and take ownership and responsibility when something isn't quite right. It's a frame of mind. Remember the power of your thoughts and beliefs; you can create abundance, or you can create scarcity. Can you believe in your heart that there really is enough? Enough time, enough energy, enough money, enough love? Can you believe that you will be okay no matter what? Can you accept yourself just the way you are? And if you want to make a change, that's okay, too. Do it with enjoyment and acceptance, rather than fear and judgment. Give to yourself what you need to make yourself happy, and then you won't have to *try* to give to others. It will come naturally.

When we are generous in the right way, we are more balanced and happier naturally. We don't have to try to be happy; we just are. No longer do we need all the mantras and affirmations to make us happy. You'll notice as you align yourself and respect yourself and others, this happens very naturally. All of a sudden you'll notice that you were happy for like, wow, three straight days, and you didn't even think about it.

We talked about it earlier. Happiness is a choice and doesn't have to be forced if we really do align ourselves and make the right choices for ourselves. We can in every moment be generous and choose happiness. Choose to be happy no matter what is happening. Commit to happiness. We're only here on this earth to be happy. Think about it. You are born, you live, and then you die. How do you want to live? With genuine generosity, there's an authentic feeling of abundance and happiness.

Before you venture into Chapter 6, take some time to reflect.

What SHIFT Will You Make?

Scan the chapter. List the topics that resonated with you.

_____

_____

Hone in on one or two areas that will make the biggest impact for you.

_____

_____

Imagine the impact. Why is this important? How will you feel when you've accomplished this?

_____

_____

Figure out your plan and how you will stay on track.

_____

_____

Take action. Start now. Schedule it now, and include your follow-up.

_____

_____

Enjoy! Remember to choose to be happy, every step of the way!

_____

_____

References

Ban Breathnach, S. (2009). *Simple Abundance*. New York, New York: Warner Books, Inc.

Chopra, D. (1994). *The Seven Spiritual Laws of Success: A practical guide to the fulfillment of your dreams*. San Rafael, California: Amber-Allen Publishing.

Freedman Spizman, R. (2002). *The Thank You Book: Hundreds of clever, meaningful, and purposeful ways to say thank you*. Active Parenting.

Institute of HeartMath. (2014). Retrieved from http://www.heartmath.org/free-services/tools-for-well-being/heartmath-appreciation-tool.html.

CHAPTER SIX

THE KEY TO EFFICIENT CHANGE

Growth is painful. Change is painful. But nothing is as painful as staying stuck where you don't belong.

—Mandy Hale

I remember one of the company's vice presidents saying to me, "That's just management theory—no one does that in practice." I was asking him about one of the classes I was taking; the subject was change management. At the time, something didn't sit right with me, and only a few years later, as I went on to study change and worked with dozens of companies, training and developing people, I could see clearly that that VP and the rest of his team should have read the book from my management class! Too late for that company—the management team's resistance to change caused its demise. Yes, they made some changes—they remodeled, they changed accounting systems, they spent money on incentivizing people to be creative—but they didn't change their thoughts, attitudes, and beliefs, so they didn't change the way they did business. Naturally, people resisted the change. I'm not sure if they ever realized in hindsight what went wrong. Sadly, that's an all-too-familiar story many have witnessed.

It's either go forward, change, and grow or be stagnant, go backward, and die. That's what happens if we don't make the changes that are necessary for our companies or for our lives. This is the crossroad: Do you want to change or not?

Heraclitus, the self-taught pioneer of wisdom (c. 535– c. 475 BCE), knew then "The only thing that's constant is change." Change is happening all around us today, arguably at a more rapid pace. Sometimes we don't choose the changes— recessions, bad weather, death—and we find ourselves resisting. Other times we feel more in control because we are driving the change: going to college, getting married, selecting a new job, making a move for a better quality life. You know what the difference is between the two? Our thoughts and beliefs. We tend to resist things that happen to us and accept the things we're in control of.

Anyway you look at it, change is growth. Change stretches our brains, and our brains actually love the exercise of change. It's what keeps us young and happy, if we embrace it rather than resist it.

You can change your thoughts and beliefs about change. Think of change as improvement, and no matter how painful, believe that it is always leading to something better. Those first few days when you start working out and your muscles are screaming—you know it's leading to something better. It may not always feel that way, but trust in the laws of nature and remember how much our thoughts and beliefs control us. "Your life does not get better by chance, it gets better by change," said Jim Rohn.

Okay, we all know that stuff happens! When something happens that you find yourself resisting, remember to stop and say,

"I chose this; I want this," even if you don't believe it and even if it sounds crazy. Remember, your mind is a tool. Convince your mind that you chose the change, and you will feel completely different. Since you can't change it once it's happened, you may as well accept it and move on. The only way to change the future is by changing the present.

Some people really believe they can't change or that others can't change. I have heard this so many times when working with people. Contrary to this brainwashing, science says we can change. We are not hard-wired. Our brains and our hearts are muscles and have the capability of being adjusted. Of course, there are some things we can't change, for example, our physical height, but there are many things we can change.

Overcoming Obstacles

If it doesn't challenge you, it won't change you.
—Fred Devito

There are obstacles that can hamper change, and I've discovered through my own self-reflection, as well as through working with thousands of others, that many of us are limited by internal fears and insecurities. Remember the 1980s film *Ghostbusters*? Well, we need to be fear-busters—we've got to search out those fears and either use them to our advantage or annihilate them! We need to identify fears that could hold us back, and implement appropriate behaviors to move us forward.

Although we constantly hear that change is something that is avoided or resisted, be careful not to assume that everyone is resistant to change all the time. There are certain times in our lives or certain things that we may be more prone to resisting. Some people roll with the weather no matter what it is, while others complain and hole up inside, waiting for a nice day. One person gets news of a terminal illness and immediately is grateful for the life that's passing, while another gets angry and resentful. You might hear about the change in the office layout and be open to it, while your buddy next door is picking apart everything they're doing.

When we find we are resisting change, we need to respect that it is natural to go through a psychological change process as we give up the old and come to either accept or reject the new. Although there are lots of reasons for resisting the change—mostly feelings of loss (of control, status, trust, faith, security, love)—there can also be underlying, deeper reasons. And there can be good reasons to not accept the change!

Change can take time, and if we have a way to guide ourselves and others through change, it makes it a whole lot easier. Respect differences in people, their experiences, their lives, and their unknown underlying reasons.

Many employees I speak with tell me it's not the change they are resisting, but how the change is rolled out. The few who are in charge are in control and enthusiastic about the change, as long as they are driving it. They don't think about how and what it takes to implement the change. Employees don't know why the change is happening, which of them it's going to affect, what might change, or if the change will be successful. Those few in charge steamroll in and implement the change, with little if any explanation or consultation. The fact is that resistance to change is an issue, especially in the workplace, because it's not being handled properly. So yes, in most companies, the top obstacle to a successful change program is employee resistance to change at all levels, including frontline personnel, middle management, and senior management. Leaders must understand how to effectively implement change—in themselves and in their team.

The Five Steps of Change™

The important thing is this: To be able at any moment to sacrifice what we are for what we could become.

—Charles Dubois

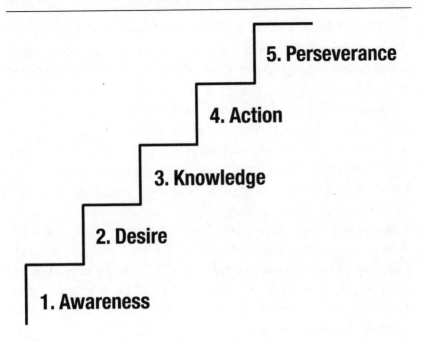

Figure 6.1. The Five Steps of Change™

Like most things, it begins with us and a belief that we can change. Having a tool to guide us makes it easier, more efficient, and more enjoyable. The Five Steps of Change™—awareness, desire, knowledge, action, and perseverance—are guaranteed to make sustainable change. (See Figure 6.1.) There is one caveat—you have to follow the steps!

Step 1: Awareness

The universe is not short on wake-up calls. We're just quick to hit the snooze button.

—Brene Brown

Change begins with awareness, and admittedly, being aware can be challenging. Are you aware that you are unaware? How do we become aware?

Think about a time when you've wanted to change. Not when someone else wanted you to change, but when you really wanted to make a change in your life. If you remember, there was a moment when you realized this. There was a moment of awareness that alerted you to your situation. Sometimes that moment of awareness we get does not come in a pleasant manner. For example, one morning as you get dressed, you realize you have gained weight because your pants are snug; or you notice a large majority of your team at work is negative and disengaged from work. Normally, when you become aware in this manner, you judge it, and then you resist the awareness and go into a blame and excuse mode: Well, it's wintertime, and I just don't have time to exercise, and everyone keeps bringing in food; or everyone is so negative, and I've tried everything to get them empowered to do their work. It's the millennium generation—they just don't care.

Awareness might come to you more positively. The opportunity comes along to be promoted to manager because you've done such a great job at work. You have an awareness that you can behave differently to get that promotion. You might visualize yourself as successful at a future goal and realize you can make a change to get there. Athletes, musicians, and many very successful people, like Richard Branson, Donald Trump, and Wayne Dyer, can see themselves in a future state, which drives them forward and makes change easier.

The type of awareness that we're talking about here is self-awareness—the ability to be aware of your own values, beliefs, thoughts, feelings, and actions. If you can be aware without judging yourself, every awareness can lead to a choice, your choice. If you could say, "Okay, I don't fit in my jeans. I know I've been eating more, and I need to make some changes to fit back into those jeans" rather than saying, "Oh, I can't believe these jeans don't fit. I hate the holidays and winter. It does this to me every year." Can you see the difference? In the first statement, you've become aware and have taken responsibility. In the second statement, you've become aware and blamed everything else and judged yourself negatively. Another example is maybe you've been told that others perceive you as rude. If you're aware with judgment, you react defensively by making excuses or blaming: "He needs to be talked to that way; it's the only way he'll listen to me!"

When we blame and make excuses, we become stuck where we are. When we judge ourselves this way, it's contrary to making any kind of positive change. If we're aware without judgment, we objectively consider the person's perception and agree or disagree. We can then decide if we want to make a change, whether it's to change our actual behavior or to change others' perceptions of our behavior.

So when you notice that your team of employees is negative and disengaged, can you imagine the difference in the thoughts that you could have? You could think, "Okay, there's negativity going on, and people are working on personal things rather than projects. Let me take a look at this to see how I've contributed and what we can do." On the other hand, your thought might be "I cannot believe how negative everyone is. It's ridiculous. I don't know what else I can do—it doesn't seem to matter. People just don't have any loyalty—they don't care about anything but themselves." Which option do you think has any chance of making a positive change?

Without being able to look objectively at yourself and your situation, it's almost impossible to focus on the right things to make change. The key to awareness when making change is to be objective about it. Don't judge and then play victim. In fact, lighten up about it. While it's important to be aware, it helps to not be too hard on yourself and to even have some fun with it. Take it from Maysoon Zayid, who is using humor to change the world: "We have to be able to be self-critical, but not to the point of being self-destructive." Being aware without judgment is necessary to keep moving up The Five Steps of Change™.

Step 2: Desire

> It's always in the want to that people discover the how to.
> —Victor E. Frankl

Changing habits begins with awareness, and desire is what gets you motivated. The desire is your want to; it's your passion, purpose, and commitment. It's your *why* or your driving force, and it comes from your heart. Without desire, change won't happen, and/or it won't last.

Once you're aware, you can then look at your motivation to make a change. You can objectively look at what it will be like if you don't make the change and what it will be like if you do make the change, rather than take it personally and get defensive about it. Is it worth it to you to make the change? Does it align with your purpose, priorities, and passions? Do you really want the change? It reminds me of that country song that says, "How bad do you want it?"

People are motivated by either pain or pleasure. Consider the person whose pants were snug. She could choose to visualize how great she will feel when she's wearing those pants again, how much energy she'll have, and how happy she'll be, or she might be more motivated by thinking about how sluggish and terrible she'll feel if she doesn't do anything and how much money she'll have to spend on new and bigger clothes. Either choice is a consequence, and if we're aware and truthful with ourselves, we'll know which motivates us.

While we're learning new things, we need to be aware of how we are reacting to the change. Are we resisting by complaining and not enjoying the growth at all, or are we embracing it by enjoying the progress we are making? Which do you think is more effective—and definitely more efficient? We learn, grow, and change faster when we believe in it, when we're aware of how we feel about it, and when we choose it because we understand the value. Not when someone else tries to force us to change.

Have you ever tried getting someone else to change? It doesn't usually turn out well, does it? Just think about a time when someone was trying to change you. Until you saw the benefit of making the change, you probably resisted or made a surface change to pacify the person—but it wasn't a genuine or lasting change. People change only when they decide to make the change themselves. We can demand, bribe, or threaten, and sometimes people do change, for a short time, but you can almost guarantee that they are holding resentment, which will cause them to sabotage themselves or revert back to the original behavior. When you're not looking, they're probably doing what they supposedly changed, complaining about you, or doing personal things because they're just not vested in it.

Should we give up on other people then? If you can't change them, I mean? Just because we cannot change people doesn't mean we cannot provide opportunities for awareness and help them see what's in it for them to change. Then it is their choice. And we need to respect their choice. There are always consequences for our choices, pain or pleasure—things that happen based on what we do.

You may not agree with their choice. Then you need to decide: Do you want to stick around this person, can you live with that, or do you want to leave or have them leave? You don't need all the drama and suffering that usually happens because you can't get the person to change. Accept it. When you respect others because you have learned to respect yourself, they will change if they want to. When you do not respect them, they may not change, sometimes just because you want them to and they are rebelling —in which case everyone loses. But make no mistake about it—you will not be changing them. They will not be changing you. We can give others the choice of change by providing the awareness, opportunity, and responsibility.

When you recognize something you really need to change and you find yourself resisting, it's a good opportunity to hold up the mirror and dig deeper. Sometimes it's just our ego trying to protect us. Sometimes it's just your habit of resisting. Do your best to be open, and ask yourself what's in it for you if you make the change. As crazy as it might sound, pretending you chose it and you want it—even though you feel like you didn't or don't—can help you accept the change.

Take the example of the manager with the awareness of his negative team and his own role in it. What will be the result if he doesn't change? Well, he may not meet his goals and could ultimately be fired, or he'll have to hire a whole new staff and hope they have better attitudes and work ethics. The latter, of course, will be very costly to do, and without changing his perspective, he is likely to see the same traits in the new employees. If he does make a change in attitude, he will probably have more motivated, productive employees and reach his goals. He'll keep his job and might even be promoted. He'll enjoy work a whole lot more. So if he accepts it, owns it, and even acts as if he chose it (or at least played a part in creating it), he can then move on to making the change. Then the question becomes what and how does he change.

Step 3: Knowledge

To know what you know and what you do not know, that is true knowledge.

—Confucius

Knowing your desire, your *why*, opens you up to accepting the *what* and the *how*. A lot of us just want to jump right into the knowledge step, where you ask, "What do I need to do and how do I do it? What does it take to make this happen?" Although you need to find the knowledge—the way—just make sure you don't skip the desire step. Desire is the emotion, the why, and it will fuel the knowledge.

Knowing the how gives us confidence and support. Knowing ourselves helps us find the way that works for us. Bear in mind that just the knowledge and motivation isn't always enough. We might need some kind of support as well—a coach, a friend, or even a support group.

One way of finding knowledge is to find someone who's been successful at what you are attempting. It's important to respect that it can be different for everyone, but it's useful to look at how others have done it. Let's go back to our examples. You want to get back into your favorite jeans. If you know someone who has gained weight and then successfully lost that weight and kept it off, you can ask him what he did. Perhaps you can hire a trainer or a coach with proven success to help you, or maybe you can get information about a diet online that's worked for lots of people. You can search and find almost anything these days. I often think, what did we do B.G.—before Google?

Take the example of the manager with the negative team. Once he's realized that he needs to change himself first, he needs to find a way to do it. There are books, executive coaches, mentors, and leadership classes. The manager's awareness and understanding of his own intent sometimes is enough without needing a class or a coach, but most of us need some help because often the behavior that needs changing is rooted in our thoughts and beliefs. This can take time, commitment, and action.

Brainstorming is a good method of getting the knowledge to help you improve. Often we know what we need to do, but we're just not objective enough to think of it. We need to get out of our own way and consider other options. Brainstorming helps us think creatively and get outside the box. First, strive to think of as many ideas as possible and not judge them. In fact, come up with crazy ideas you'd probably never use. This will help your brain stretch to think of things you haven't thought of yet. Once you feel like you have a large selection of ideas, then you can start narrowing them down by crossing some off and combining ideas. A good brainstorming session will undoubtedly create new solutions.

While knowledge is an important step, knowing how isn't enough. Knowledge has to be put into action and reviewed for effectiveness.

Step 4: Action

Well done is better than well said.

—Benjamin Franklin

We now have an awareness of something we want to change. We do the research or get knowledge on how to change—and then we don't do it. When it comes to taking action, many people stall or never get started. They get the knowledge they need, and then nothing happens. Why? Think of times in your life when you've gathered the knowledge you needed, perhaps you read a book or took a class, and then you didn't do anything with it. Let's use a previous example. The manager who knows what he needs to do to be a more effective leader but is not doing it. He may not take the action because deep down he's worried he will not be successful, and it will be apparent that he's not a good manager. Or it seems overwhelming and he gets stuck with how to start. Perhaps he is not staying aligned to his priorities, and too burned out to focus on it. There are many reasons people do not take action, and most of them boil down to that four-letter F word that keeps messing us up—fear! There's something holding us back.

Maybe it's your thoughts and beliefs you need to take action on first. Start writing and saying those mantras like it's your business. Read more self-help and inspiring books to give your subconscious the fuel it needs to drive positive behavior.

Have you ever noticed that a lot of us get in our own way? For some reason, we make it harder than it has to be, or we sabotage ourselves.

Fear isn't always obvious, and if we're not practicing awareness, it can be very difficult to even recognize fear. The fears we have are directly linked to the beliefs we have. Sometimes fear can be an opportunity for awareness, so fear isn't always a negative thing. In fact, if we are practicing true awareness, we're not judging the fear, and we're not playing victim. When we learn to recognize fear, understand where it is coming from, and move on, fear becomes a trigger to help us. And we can respect it.

For years, I struggled with health and weight. The health issues were never diagnosed, but the symptoms were like allergies and led to chronic sinus infections. My weight, although only 10 or 20 pounds over my desired weight, made me feel sluggish, and I didn't have as much energy. I tried one diet and exercise program after the other. I always lost the weight and felt better, but then I eventually slipped back to where I had been before.

This did not change for me until two very important people in my life had health-related issues that first made me fearful for them and then made me respect what I needed to do. My grandson was diagnosed with acid reflux at nine months old and prescribed an adult dose of Prevacid. My daughter refused to accept the medicine and sought out an alternative way to heal him. Through healthy eating, not only was he healed in 30 days, but she was the healthiest she had ever been!

My father was diagnosed with squamous cell carcinoma around the same time, and that led me to research healthy eating like my daughter had done. By supporting him, juicing and eating healthy, I began to feel better than I'd ever felt. My symptoms disappeared, and it was pretty obvious to me that processed food was the guilty party.

Not allowing fear to paralyze you but having a healthy respect for it and for consequences can propel you into action. To make any kind of change, we need to take action. Take a step and make a plan, even if it's just a small step. Again, we ought not judge ourselves, but just do the best we can to actually do something. Judging ourselves blocks us from making change. Don't wait for perfection—it's like waiting for something that will never arrive. Act on the knowledge. Revisit your desire.

Taking action is about practicing what we learn until it becomes a habit.

For example, while I'm learning to play the drums, I don't just read about it and watch others drum. I have to get those sticks in my hands and play! Malcolm Gladwell has shared the "10,000-Hour Rule," claiming that the key to success is practice: practicing a specific task for a total of around 10,000 hours. While I fully believe in practice, my unverified theory is that you won't need as many hours because you'll have more energy when you really have the desire, the passion, and the best method possible (a great coach or teacher, book, or class).

If you feel stuck, hire that coach to help you be a better manager or lose weight. *Try* is not in the vocabulary—it's all about doing. For example, practice the new leadership skill you've been taught—to listen and help problem-solve—rather than just tell your employees what to do. Practice and practice until you feel comfortable with it. And even then, be aware that like diets, exercise, and any other change we start, it's easy to get off track.

Step 5: Perseverance

In the confrontation between the stream and the rock, the stream always wins—not through strength but by perseverance.

—H. Jackson Brown

Maybe you take action, and you fall flat on your face. You feel like you've failed. You decide to eat healthy food and exercise, so you can fit into those jeans, and after three days, you cave and eat cake. As Tigger says, "Life is not about how fast you run or how high you climb, but how well you bounce."

Get up, shake it off, keep going. Try something different. Just don't judge it and get stuck in the negative. When you get off track, be aware of it, and don't be so hard on yourself. Look at it objectively, think about what happened and how you can do it better in the future, and let it go. Remind yourself of your motivation. Just keep doing your best in every situation. Typically the change you desire won't happen overnight. Be patient. Persevere. We might need to course-correct, change methods, get more help, and revisit our desire to get motivated again. But never give up!

The secret of change is to focus all of your energy, not on fighting the old, but on building the new.

—Socrates

In Chapter 1, we talked about being positive and choosing happiness. Sometimes it's difficult; some situations make it very challenging. Let's see how The Five Steps of Change™ can guide us to choosing happiness.

Awareness: As soon as you're aware of your emotions, you can just say, "Interesting, I'm feeling down right now."

Desire: Then you can ask yourself how you want to feel. This is where you get to choose. Yes, it's that simple. Do I want to be happy or not? If I really want to be happy, I can explore the next step of how, the knowledge.

Knowledge: How do we just be happy? The first step is just choosing in that moment to see the positive. Another thing I do is make sure I'm feeding myself positive thoughts and staying focused on them. Again, our minds need to be managed, not left roaming around negatively. I think of managing our thoughts as equivalent to dieting, exercise, education, and practice.

Action: Take some action steps. Make a habit of reading and watching uplifting things to keep your thoughts positive.

Perseverance: When I get off track, I surround myself with positive people, I eat healthy, and I exercise. I get back to reading positive things. You have to figure out what works best for you.

I share this example of choosing happiness because it's one of the things that has made the biggest difference in my own life. I'm grateful, and I want to pass this gift along to anyone who is ready and willing to take it!

Remaining aware through every step will help you stay on track, and lightening up a bit will help you enjoy the journey. Recognize your hard work, and appreciate your opportunity to change. Go with it, rather than resist it. Choose happiness. Have fun with it—the energy and enthusiasm will be contagious. Enjoy and celebrate.

Leading with GRIT® inevitably requires some adjustments in your life and your workplace. Change is happening at such a rapid pace within our organizations that if we don't manage it properly, the people who resist change can create more wasted time and loss of productivity than almost anything else. Resistance is very hard to track and measure, making it easily ignored or not managed properly. As you're looking to change systems, change office space, change anything at work—be aware of yourself and your situation—consider your players and manage your team. Be mindful of why this change is important—your desire. Research, so you know the best method. Take action and keep going, with debriefings and follow-ups along the way.

Changing habits and clearing blocks are crucial to a successful transition, within ourselves and within our organizations. The Five Steps of Change™ guides us through the transition. Awareness, desire, knowledge, action, and perseverance provide inspiration and patience for making sustainable change in your life.

As you begin reading Parts II and III, The Five Steps of Change™ will help you navigate the changes you desire, creating the workplace and life you deserve. Enjoy the journey!

Before you venture into Chapter 7, take some time to reflect.

What SHIFT Will You Make?

Scan the chapter. List the topics that resonated with you.

_____

_____

Hone in on one or two areas that will make the biggest impact for you.

_____

_____

Imagine the impact. Why is this important? How will you feel when you've accomplished this?

_____

_____

Figure out your plan and how you will stay on track.

_____

_____

Take action. Start now. Schedule it now, and include your follow-up.

_____

_____

Enjoy! Remember to choose to be happy, every step of the way!

_____

_____

PART II

COMMUNICATING WITH GRIT®

In Part I we focused on individual development of GRIT® to provide the foundation we need to improve our relationships at work and beyond. Now in Part II we will focus on communicating with GRIT®—making communication easier, more enjoyable, and more productive.

Part III will guide us through the impact we make at work.

CHAPTER SEVEN

CAN YOU HEAR ME NOW?

Courage is what it takes to stand up and speak; courage is also what it takes to sit down and listen.

—Winston Churchill

After two days of training, the last thing I felt like doing was talking with the driver on the way to the airport. So as I collapsed into the seat, I listened, at first maybe halfheartedly, while watching all the traffic in Brooklyn and trying to keep my eyes open. Then, as I picked up on a few words, I began to understand his broken English, and I found myself very present in his story. He was sharing the problems his son was having with drugs and alcohol and how difficult it was not being from this country and trying to find the help he needed. I could relate to his story, as one of my brothers was experiencing a similar problem, and even being a citizen, it was difficult for

my brother to get successful rehabilitation and
support. And so I listened, for well over an hour,
hardly saying a word, except to nod my head, raise
my eyebrows, and furrow my brow to show that I
understood, and empathized. When we arrived at the
airport and I asked how much, he replied, "No, no.
No charge." I was shocked, and because usually
nothing is free in New York, with hesitation and a bit
of fear, I said, "Oh no, I insist." Still shaking his head,
he very gracefully said, "Best conversation I've ever
had—please, no charge." Wow—talk about
generosity!

When we are completely present and listening with our
hearts, it is a gift to those on the receiving end. This is
pure generosity, and it sets the law of giving and receiving in
motion, as we saw with the driver. Because many people don't
receive enough of this kind of listening, it's safe to say that most
of us could improve our listening skills, especially within the
relationships that are most important to us.

As we dug into GRIT® in Part I, we discovered that
when we know our priorities, and we stay aligned, we respect
ourselves and others and are generous in the right places.
Listening is a prime example, and crucial for any relationship.
Subscribers to the *Harvard Business Review* rated the ability to communicate "the most important fact in making an
executive promotable." They ranked it more important than
ambition, education, and hard work (Groysberg and Slind,
2012). Listening is instrumental to effective communication.
The average business executive spends a large amount of time
communicating with people. Can you guess what the biggest
complaint of employees is? That's right—the boss doesn't effectively listen. "They tell more than they ask, they aren't present,
they don't acknowledge that they heard me, and they don't
follow up."

Listening could very well be the most valuable skill in any relationship. It's definitely one of the most underutilized. Maybe that's why God gave us two ears and one mouth, as the saying goes—we're suppose to use them in that proportion.

Wasted meeting time, unhappy customers, confused employees, and lost sales are only some of the costs of ineffective listening. Imagine this scenario: A salesperson attends an internal meeting that he believes is a waste of time, and he misses important information about a new product. Later in a client meeting, he fails to listen to the client's underlying needs, which would have been met with the new product (that he doesn't know about because he wasn't listening). The customer leaves the meeting unsatisfied and chooses a different vendor. This is just one example of how ineffective listening affects the bottom line.

Barriers

There are always distractions, if you allow them.
—Tony La Russa

It's said that on average we receive around 1,800 messages each day via e-mail, text, face-to-face, instant messaging, Facebook, and telephone, among many other avenues. How do you decide what you're going to listen to? Keeping our attention focused in the right places and not getting distracted can be extremely challenging.

Consider a typical day for yourself. How often do you think you tune out and you're not really listening? Instead, you find yourself judging whether you like or dislike what's being said, or you're deciding if you agree or disagree, or you think you already know what the other person is going to say.

It's not always easy to listen. We get distracted, not only by people and technology but even by words. We hear a word, and then our mind goes to a thought triggered from that word, and pretty soon we're not listening. Or we start to think about what we need to say, and we tune out. We stop listening and start formulating our rebuttal. In addition, we have preconceived notions, prior experiences, and personal agendas that cause us to discount what is being said.

Considering that we listen to people at a rate of 125 to 250 words per minute, while we think at 1,000 to 3,000 words per minute, it's no wonder we tune out!

Here are some of the most common barriers to listening:

- Our own attitude about what we are going to hear or the person who is delivering the message.
- Assumptions about the person's motives for what they are saying.
- Distractions: physical or mental/emotional.
- Taking things personally.
- Lack of trust or credibility.
- Getting excited about something the person said, and you start thinking of how it relates to you, and what you want to say, "Oh, me, too" and take over the conversation rather than listen.
- Trying to remember a person's name or some other fact you think you should know.
- They're not speaking fast enough, so I fill in for them.
- Not taking the time. Our lives are so busy, it's hard to clear our minds and be present.
- Competition: trying to one-up someone and so not listening fully to what they are saying.

Take a moment to scan through that list one more time, this time with an awareness of your own tendencies. Just be aware.

Think about how you feel when someone's not listening to you—when they don't make eye contact, when they are multitasking, looking around, not giving you their full attention. Even when you're on the telephone, you know when the other person has checked out for a moment. You know it by the split-second hesitation or the tone of voice when the person responds. Most of us agree it doesn't feel good when you're not being listened to. It can feel like the person doesn't respect you.

In some relationships, you might speak up and let the person know when you notice that they are not listening. Unfortunately, this doesn't always impact the person because although you've pointed it out, their behavior won't shift until their thoughts and beliefs change. Most likely, it has developed into a bad habit over time, and they're not even aware they are doing it. Once they're aware, remember The Five Steps of Change™, they need to have a desire to change, and they may need to change habits (actions) as well.

In other relationships, perhaps with a boss or coworker, you may not even speak up when that person isn't listening to you. You walk away feeling disenchanted with the person, and most of the time they don't even realize. Later, you're not as engaged with them, and they have no idea why.

When people aren't listening, you notice they have that deer-in-the-headlight look, or they interrupt as if you weren't even talking, perhaps sidetracking by taking over with their own story. It goes something like this.

At dinner, your friend Michelle is telling you about her vacation in Italy, and she mentions a wonderful gift she found for her son while there. You jump in with "Oh, how is Jackson, is he doing okay after the separation?" and bam, just like that, the conversation is all about Jackson—his kids, the poor guy not getting custody, which then leads to a discussion of the unfairness of custody laws, and well, before long, it's time to go home, and you have seen only two photos of Michelle's trip to Italy.

This kind of sidetracking happens often in conversations. Our questions lead the speaker away from where she was going to where we want to go. Depending on the topic and the relationship, you might lead the speaker back, but often we don't. And for most of us who experience this as the speaker, it doesn't feel like our friend really cares to hear about our vacation. The intent isn't bad; people just get distracted and forget the purpose of the conversation.

As soon as you notice you've taken your discussion off course, just bring it back with a simple statement like "It was good to catch up on Jackson. Now tell me more about Italy! I want to see those pictures and hear all about it!"

Think of the wasted time and dollars in business meetings and even informal workplace conversations when the topic gets sidetracked. Effective listening includes staying on course. Barriers to listening can be extremely costly to an organization or to any relationship.

It Takes More Than Your Ears

Attention is the rarest and purest form of generosity.

—Simon Weil

With GRIT®, we are tuned in and listening with respect, and we keep focused on the person. We listen for the full truth, and we give our undivided attention to receive what they are saying. Our intent is to understand. We don't have to agree with what the person is saying, but if our full attention is there and we know the purpose is to understand, we can stay focused on what they are saying. And we can respond accordingly.

It has been said that 93 percent of a message someone receives is from everything other than the words: voice tone, inflection, intonation, body language, facial expressions, and the like. The actual words make up only about 7 percent of the message. Broken down, we derive approximately 55 percent of a message's meaning from the speaker's facial expressions, 38 percent from how he says the message, and 7 percent from the actual words spoken.

Although this research of Albert Mehrabian's (1972) was based around attitudes and feelings, I personally find these statistics helpful when communicating in most situations, but especially when we need to connect and relate to others. Of course, everyone takes in information differently. We take in information through all our senses, but we have our preferences. Some people are more auditory, and they digest information easiest through their ears. Others prefer visuals: They want to read and see to understand information. Some are more kinesthetic; they want to get their hands on it and try it. Regardless of our preferred way of taking in information, it can't be denied that what a lot of people are really hearing is from your nonverbals. We listen with more than our ears—we are listening with our eyes and other senses as well. We're taking in all the clues and putting it together to make sense of what someone is saying.

Understand the Why

The biggest communication problem is we do not listen to understand. We listen to reply.

—Anonymous

We're expected to listen a lot in our lives, yet we've had little, if any, good training on how to effectively listen. Most of us did not have a class on listening in high school or college. In fact, I've read it's less than 2 percent of us who have any formal education on how to listen. We were taught to read and write, and some of us had public speaking. And while our parents were constantly telling us to listen, what they really meant was obey. I'm pretty sure we heard and understood what our parents were saying; we just chose not to do it. In a lot of cases, we think of listening as more than just hearing. Often when we expect someone to listen, we want them to understand what we are saying and what we are asking them to do, and we also expect them to take action on it. Interestingly, this might be why it's so challenging for some people to just listen and empathize. They've been so conditioned to take action that they are constantly thinking they're suppose to do something, solve something, or fix something, and they usually jump in too quickly to do so. Meanwhile, that other person just wanted to be heard and understood.

When you are listening, clarify the speaker's purpose, so you know what you are listening for and if there is any intended action. Is their purpose to inform you of something, persuade you to do something, to teach you something, to give you directions, or to just get you to lend an ear? If we know why the person wants us to listen, it will help us know how to listen and what to do or not do. Check in with them: "Hey, you just need to vent right now, or do you want me to help you figure out what to do?"

If we are mindful of how we should listen, it will help us prepare to listen appropriately. For example, we can pretend we're going to be quizzed on what this person is saying. It might sound silly, but it will help us keep focused on all the words and the nonverbals. On the quiz, we'll have to report the purpose and what we're suppose to do as a result.

When we do tune out, just fess up. Most likely the person knows anyway. Say, "I'm sorry, my mind just took a trip. Can you repeat that last thing after (xyz) that you said?" Not only will you get to hear what you missed but you'll also build trust through your integrity.

In almost all listening situations, the goal is to at least understand what is being said. You may have heard the term *reflective listening*. Reflective listening is when you paraphrase back what you think you heard, so the person talking can either confirm or correct your perception. It shows the person that you are striving to comprehend what was said. "So you want me to do the labor report first, then get the payroll out, even if people's checks will be late?" The boss replies, "Oh, no, I'm sorry. I meant after payroll. The labor report is your first priority after payroll. Thanks for clarifying."

Reflective listening starts by getting yourself ready to listen, physically and mentally. Enter conversations with an open mind and with a positive intent. Be silent at first. I love that *listen* and *silent* are spelled with the same letters—it's a great way to remember to be silent. Get comfortable with silence. Don't jump in too quickly. It sends the message that you're not fully listening. Summarize or paraphrase what you heard to clarify the message with the person. Ask questions to get more information, and stay focused on the topic, so you can better understand what is being said. Be aware of your thoughts and feelings—consciously put them on hold until you are finished listening.

Empathy

Eventually you come to realize that most people aren't looking for a fight but for someone to surrender to.

—Robert Brault

There will be times when you will need to take reflective listening to the next level—to empathic listening. Here, you'll do all the steps of reflective listening, and you will also check for understanding of the emotions behind the speaker's words. Keep in mind you'll often *hear* more through nonverbals.

By checking for understanding of emotions, you are taking it one step further to empathize with others. You are listening for their emotion and reflecting back what you think the person is feeling. "It seems like you're frustrated with the whole thing, huh?" Just letting the person know that you are tuned into the emotion builds a stronger connection. It wouldn't be good to *tell* the other person what they are feeling, but rather check in with more of a questioning tone, so the person can confirm or correct your perception. Empathic listening is a great way to who respect and build trust. It shows you care enough to be in tune to how a person is feeling. It is foundational to leadership, coaching, problem solving, and enhancing relationships.

The need for leaders to be able to connect with, relate to, and appreciate people is only increasing, and it's resulting in organizations spending time and money on developing skills such as empathy. Dan Pink in his book *A Whole New Mind* (Pink, 2006) cites creativity and empathy as two of the top skills needed in the workplace today. Dan Goleman in his book *Emotional Intelligence* (Goleman, 2005) argues that noncognitive skills, such as empathy, can matter as much as IQ.

Whether for the workplace or in our personal lives, empathy is an important skill, and it doesn't come naturally for all of us. The good news is that we can develop it. As we know from the Five Steps of Change™, that means awareness, desire, knowledge, action, and perseverance. If you're aware and you want to improve your empathy, it's just a matter of how, and then practice it.

To practice empathy, here are a couple of things you can do. Take some time to do some people watching. Pay attention to people's facial expressions, and see if you can identify the emotions they are feeling. Although you might not want to check in with them to see if you are correct, it's good practice to just try to name them. It helps you to be more mindful of emotions and focus more attention there. You can also practice with your family, although you might let them know that you're doing this; otherwise, they could wonder what the heck is going on with you. So just check in with how they are feeling. In your own mind or in a conversation with them, guess the emotion. Another way to practice empathy is to watch a movie without sound and name the emotions you are seeing expressed on people's faces. See if you can relate to or understand what they might be feeling.

Parents and teachers can help children to identify and name their emotions and to consider the feelings of other people. Just by talking about it with them, children will learn empathy. They will be less stressed and confused individuals who will be able to connect and communicate much more effectively.

We obviously don't need to use empathic listening in all situations, but in my experience, it's the one that is lacking the most. Empathic listening will enhance relationships by creating stronger connections and building trust.

Choose When to Listen

It's not about "having" time. It's about making time.

—Anonymous

Should we always drop everything and listen to anyone who demands it? I've heard many executives say that they purposely don't listen attentively because they don't want their office to become like a therapist's couch. They witness a colleague taking too many interruptions while being completely frustrated. It's obvious the colleague is feeling that he can't control the traffic into his office. So the executives avoid listening altogether because they don't want this to happen to them.

Actually, if you are listening to everyone and everything, you aren't practicing GRIT®. You are not staying aligned to what's most important. You are not respecting yourself or the other person. You most likely end up pretending to listen or being rude, which isn't showing respect or integrity, either. We have to manage our situations and not allow someone to take up too much of our time.

I'll never forget my daughter at 13, coming home from school and talking a mile a minute. Meanwhile, I'm on the computer, glancing and nodding only sporadically at her with a blank look in my eyes—trying to work and listen at the same time. Calling me right out, she looked me in the eyes and said, "Either listen, or don't!" Although she could have delivered this message better, she was absolutely right. It is more respectful to let a person know that you cannot listen right now than pretending to listen.

The thing is that in a lot of situations a person won't tell you like my daughter did. A customer or a direct report may not feel comfortable or feel like it's their responsibility to call you out when you're not listening. We know that not listening will have negative repercussions, but often we never trace it back to our poor listening. Or by the time we know, it's too late. An owner of an information technology service company was talking to me about her need for training, and this was exactly the example she used. A prospect had replied to her, letting her know that they would be going with a competitor, due to the lack of attention given by her salesperson. While the prospect was most likely irritated by the salesperson, you can see how it does not get brought up during the interaction. Only later might we hear about it.

Awareness and practicing being present will help you naturally stay more in tune. Having a foundation of GRIT® will keep you aligned and focused in the right ways. For example, if we find that we can't listen right now, we simply let the person know: "I'm sorry, Anne, it's not a good time. I won't be able to give you my full attention. Can we talk about this later?"

While it's each person's choice if they want to listen—and there will be consequences either way—it's a leader's responsibility to make time for listening. It helps employees feel acknowledged, recognized, and important so they engage and stay aligned. When a leader is good at listening, she will gain information she couldn't have gotten elsewhere. By practicing GRIT®, listening becomes easier. There is less effort. You do it because you want to, not because you have to. You manage your conversations appropriately.

As you delve into Chapter 8 and explore what messages you are sending, keep this acronym in mind: LAF—listen, acknowledge, and follow through. Just think, "LAF with people," and you will continue to build trust and enhance engagement. When you invest time upfront by listening effectively, there will be exponential positive results to your relationships and your bottom line.

Before you venture into Chapter 8, take some time to reflect.

What SHIFT Will You Make?

Scan the chapter. List the topics that resonated with you.

_____

_____

Hone in on one or two areas that will make the biggest impact for you.

_____

_____

Imagine the impact. Why is this important? How will you feel when you've accomplished this?

_____

_____

Figure out your plan and how you will stay on track.

_____

_____

Take action. Start now. Schedule it now, and include your follow-up.

_____

_____

Enjoy! Remember to choose to be happy, every step of the way!

_____

_____

References

Goleman, D. (2005). *Emotional Intelligence: Why it can matter more than IQ.* New York, New York: Bantam Dell.

Groysberg, B., Slind, M. (2012). Leadership Is a Conversation. Harvard Business Review. Retrieved from https://hbr.org/2012/06/leadership-is-a-conversation.

Mehrabian, A. (1972). *Silent Messages: Implicit communication of emotions and attitudes.* Belmont, California: Wadsworth Publishing Company.

Pink, D. (2006). *A Whole New Mind: Why right-brainers will rule the future.* New York, New York: Penguin Group.

CHAPTER EIGHT

WHAT MESSAGE ARE YOU SENDING?

Never separate the life you live from the words you speak.

—Paul Wellstone

As Sally walked into the office, her manager, Justin, barely making eye contact, called her over by condescendingly motioning with his finger. "What is this?" he barked. Sally tried to explain as he curtly handed the report to her. Without any further eye contact and rather sarcastically, he said, "Try again."

Infuriated, Sally sat staring at her computer for about 30 minutes, unable to focus or concentrate on what she was supposed to be doing. As her friend and coworker Carol passed by, Sally asked if she had a minute. Forty-five minutes later, Carol and Sally had hashed over the situation and bashed Justin enough that if thoughts could kill, he'd be dead on the floor. Of course, Sally's anger was fueled by the conversation, and although she went back to work, her mind wasn't in it, let alone her heart.

Sally ended up making a costly mistake on another project that day, and she spent nearly double the time as she found herself struggling to stay focused. On top of it all, she received a phone call from a customer while she was trying to catch up on her work, and because of the edge in Sally's voice, the customer hung up irritated and ended up looking elsewhere.

Let's say Sally makes $30 an hour. Add up all the wasted time and errors and the customer's decision to leave, taking a large chunk of business away, and it's fair to say this manager just cost the company easily $150,000 with a 1-minute interaction that could have gone so differently.

We'll never know all the lost revenue, stress, illness, and residual mistakes that are caused by ineffective communication. It's costly because if you're not measuring it, you're not paying attention to it. It's almost impossible to track the full impact of ineffective communication. We'll never really know the extent of the damage it causes. It's like carpenter ants eating away at your house. You see only one or two ants, but when the wall gets knocked down to repair a board, 10,000 ants come racing out and the damage is tenfold. If you don't see a rotting board and catch it early enough, you may not see the damage until the house collapses.

While listening skills are critical to communication, equally important is the message you send. Since beliefs are internal and invisible to the outside world, words and actions are the only tools we have to communicate these beliefs and inspire trust. When we improve our messaging, listening becomes easier for others. It's a win-win.

I find it ironic that we're supposed to have the most sophisticated communication system of all animals, and quite frankly, we're not so good at it. We avoid saying what we really should say, we don't listen with the intention of understanding, we judge what someone is saying, and we start arguing before we even understand. We don't have to like or agree with everything, but if we could just reach a level of understanding, there would be a lot less miscommunication and negative drama.

Our messages get misconstrued through the many different time zones, geographies, competing priorities and time, genders, generations, ethnicities, and cultures. There can be silos and turf issues, hidden agendas, or lack of trust or respect that distorts our message. And we can send mixed messages with opposing words and nonverbals.

With GRIT®, we are more mindful of the messages we send. We're thinking about what the other person is receiving. We strive to provide the truth, use the best method to communicate, think of everything the person may need to know, and say it the best way we can, so they can hear it. Our intent is to help, and, hey, maybe we can lighten up and give the gift of laughter to help people relax and enjoy life a bit more.

Speak Their DiSC® Language

Let your speech always be with grace, as though seasoned with salt, so that you will know how you should respond to each person.

—Colossians 4:6

Paying attention to people and adapting to talk their language will help people understand our message. One very effective tool is the DiSC® assessment mentioned earlier. Quite a few years back, I was training a group in DiSC® when one of the participants said in a joking voice, "I wish everyone could be just like me." This opened up a rich discussion on the value of having different behavioral styles in the workplace and of the challenges when it comes to communicating. Not only understanding but also appreciating all styles and adapting our communication is crucial to success.

Each of the four behavioral styles represented by DiSC®—Dominance, Influence, Steadiness, and Consciousness—has preferences or tendencies. When we understand our own priorities and preferences, we see how some things come very naturally to us, while other things take more focus and energy. With this awareness and a desire to communicate more effectively, we can adapt our approach to others. It's not about changing who we are; it's about changing our language and our approach, so the other person can understand us.

The following DiSC® image (Figure 8.1) shows the four styles and their tendencies: fast-paced and outspoken versus cautious and reflective, and questioning and skeptical versus accepting and warm.

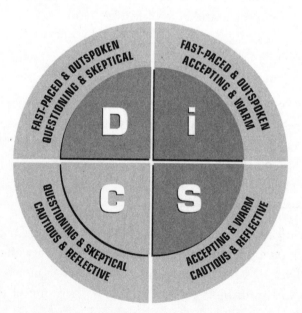

Figure 8.1. DiSC® Styles and Tendencies

If we consider a person's DiSC® tendencies, communication will improve. For example, perhaps you're talking with someone who is very fast-paced and questioning, but you prefer to be more cautious about a topic and reflect longer before you blurt out the answer. Rather than be silent while you're thinking, you can adapt by telling the person you want to think about this before answering. By speaking up, you help the fast-paced, questioning person understand what you are doing in your silence, and he is more apt to be patient.

While I was working with a group of supervisors in the U.S. Navy, one seasoned supervisor approached me on the break and said he couldn't believe how simply DiSC® broke it down and sorted it all out for him. He went on to share how clear he was now on his natural approach versus how he might need to speak a different language, depending on the person. He admitted he always felt that he had his way of communicating, and he noticed other people had their way. But he didn't ever consider that he should adapt to them.

While it's good to understand DiSC® styles, it's important to respect that people are a mix of DiSC® styles. DiSC® is not meant to label people but rather to be used as a tool to effectively adapt in the moment, to communicate more effectively.

Actions Speak Louder Than Words

Listen to a person when they look at you, not just when they talk to you.

—Anonymous

Indeed, your nonverbal communication is sending messages more powerful than the words you use, as we saw in Chapter 7. Eye contact and other body movement, as well as the physical space we occupy, help us see why truth, integrity, and respect play such a vital role. The improvements you are making with GRIT® pay off immensely when it comes to your message. Consider the message Justin sent to Sally, not even in the words, just in his nonverbal communication. By not making eye contact and motioning to her with a finger, he came across as condescending to Sally. And then when he cut her off, didn't listen, and handed her the paper back, Sally felt he was rude and disrespectful. As you can imagine, Sally told Carol a lot more of what she felt about Justin that we won't mention here!

Do you realize what messages you are sending with your nonverbals? Just think of the energy you put out when you're cynical, in a bad mood, upset with someone, frustrated, angry, or just irritated and tired. Put yourself there for a moment and pay attention to your body. It changes. It's heavy. It's low. It's closed. It's repelling. Imagine the nonverbal message you are sending. Just think about the look on your face and your body posture.

Now switch for a moment to how you are when you are feeling awesome, you couldn't be happier, you're thrilled about life, and you're feeling very grateful and alive. Now pay attention to your body. It's lighter. It's higher. It's open. It's attracting. Your nonverbals are completely different.

We have the ability to adjust; it just takes awareness and desire. How do you know you are being negative, for example? Pay attention to how you feel. Then ask yourself, "Do I want to be this way?" If not, adjust and be positive!

We're not always aware of the nonverbal messages we are sending, and sometimes they're not what we are intending. I remember one time when I was driving down the road, deep in thought, and my daughter asked me what was the matter. I caught a glimpse of my face in the rearview mirror and realized I was frowning very heavily. I looked upset. Interesting, because my thoughts weren't really upsetting to me—I think I was just so heavily in thought that my face was all squinched up that way. I laughed and replied, "Nothing, I'm just thinking, and it hurts!"

Whether our nonverbals are reflecting what we're thinking and feeling or not, if we're in integrity and respecting that others are not mind readers, we'll be careful what we are putting out there nonverbally. Even when you don't have any expression, as is often the case with someone who has a lot of C behavior in the DiSC® model, that can be misunderstood as not caring, aloof, or even angry. When people don't have enough information, they automatically fill it in. Respect that people do have perceptions, and they read and interpret body language—right or wrong. We need to do our best to fill in the truth for them. We can help send a clear message by being aware of our own facial expressions, body language, and even the words we use.

Choose Your Words Wisely

The difference between the right word and the almost right word is the difference between lightning and a lightning bug.

—Mark Twain

Words are simply labels we use to identify things, and they have different meanings to different people. Respecting this fact helps us not attach too strongly to the meaning of a word, and we can be open to consider other ways of looking at a word. Our words are tools, and we can use them to be helpful, or we can use them to hurt.

Selecting the words that keep you in integrity and respect is key to successful relationships at work and elsewhere. The words we use affect our own mood, as well as others'. Like our nonverbal communication, what comes out of our mouths is typically a direct reflection of how we feel. How do you think Justin was feeling by observing his message? He most likely was frustrated, maybe even with things other than work, and his words, or lack thereof, were far from helpful. "What is this?" and "Try again" don't really say anything helpful. Coupled with the sarcasm, it was quite hurtful. It would have taken Justin maybe 10 seconds to be mindful of the message he was sending, choose words, and change his voice tone to be helpful.

Have you ever noticed how a word can be emotionally charged? In addition to some of the obvious swear words, absolutes like *always* and *never* can push our buttons. "You're always late." "You never take out the trash." When we use absolutes, we label people. That kind of message typically puts people on the defensive. While they're trying to defend that they aren't always that way, they won't even be able to listen to you.

The word *but* can also be problematic because it negates what you just said and also can put people on the defensive. "I like what you did here but . . . " We're just waiting for the hammer to drop. Try replacing the word *but* with *and*. "I like what you did here, and it would be even better if you added more color." Or you can leave the word out: "I like what you did here. Could you add more color?"

Do you ever find yourself saying things like "I *have* to do this?" Take away "have to" and just say, "I am doing this." Or better yet, "I *get* to do this." What message does it send when we say, "I have to do this," rather than "I am doing this" or "I get to do this?" That's right, the message is that we are victims, that we have no choice, that we are being forced. Victim language happens when you're hanging out on the bottom rungs of that Accountability Ladder we explored in Chapter 3. Sometimes it's just a matter of habit, but often the words we are using are an indication of how we feel.

Certain words tend to carry more negative meanings. When we think about the messages we might be telling ourselves—with our thoughts—we can see how a thought turns into words and spirals into negative actions, which then show up as real-life problems.

Consider this list of words and phrases that you might want to avoid:

I can't

I'll try

You never

You always

But

I have to

I need

I should

Could be better (or any other negative greeting)

Instead, use words and phrases like "I will" and "I am," and tone down absolutes to be more accurate representations ("You were late three times last week and twice the week before"). Remember to replace *but* with *and* or just get rid of the *but*.

What's Missing with E-messages

Don't type at me in that tone of voice.

—Anonymous

Words become even more important when we don't have nonverbal communication to accompany them. Most of us have experienced misunderstandings when we're using e-mails, text messages, and instant messaging. Without voice tone and intonation or facial expressions and body language, we tend to fill in information that's not there. We make assumptions about the person's intent, and we take more things personally. It's almost comical how much just intonation can change the meaning of a sentence. Consider the different meanings of this sentence:

She isn't flying to New Zealand tomorrow. *She isn't, but someone is.*

She **isn't** flying to New Zealand tomorrow. *It's not true.*

She isn't **flying** to New Zealand tomorrow. *She might be taking a boat.*

She isn't flying **to** New Zealand tomorrow. *She's flying back from New Zealand.*

She isn't flying to **New Zealand** tomorrow. *She's flying somewhere else.*

She isn't flying to New Zealand **tomorrow**. *She's flying next week.*

Even when the words don't change, by changing the tone or intonation in a sentence, the whole meaning changes. No wonder we have so many misunderstandings with electronic communication! Keeping this in mind, we can pay close attention to the words we use in our electronic communications and use any relevant formatting, such as bold and italics, to help clarify our intent.

I hear so many complaints about e-mail and other e-communications while working with people in organizations. It's not the e-mail. E-mail is just a tool. It's the way we are using it. If you need something fastened with a screw, you're not going to use a hammer. Often we use e-mail or text when an in-person visit or phone call would be a lot more effective. You can always follow up with an e-mail. Anything that needs clarifying or that is emotional should be talked out first. If you feel the need to CYA (cover your arse), then follow up with an e-mail that indicates what you heard and what you agreed upon.

Other pet peeves with e-mailing include leaving people out, copying too many people in, and replying to everyone when it's not necessary. One of my clients was just telling me that she gets so many e-mails that when she gets one that is "reply all" or one that does not address her specifically, she tends to skip over those.

They do not get her attention. E-mails that are too wordy or too long often do not get read. Keep the basic GRIT® principles in mind when you craft your e-mail. Know the purpose of your message and if e-mail is appropriate. If it is, articulate it for your audience. Send it only to those involved, and stay on topic. Keep it short and to the point, while providing all the necessary information.

Communicate with Confidence

Be humble in your confidence yet courageous in your character.

—Melanie Koulouris

There are times when we need our message to come across with more confidence. Perhaps you are asking for a raise, or you're trying to convince the board that this is the best project to vote for. The words we choose and our nonverbal communication will support or detract from our message.

When you need to be more confident, start your sentences with the subject, not with you and your thoughts. For example, "I think it's time we spoke up and told him how we feel" turns into "It's time we spoke up and told him how we feel." As much as possible, get rid of the word *try* and just say you'll do it; that shows commitment. *Try* gives you a way out, an excuse. "I will try to be there" becomes "I will be there." Do you notice the difference in the level of commitment?

Pay attention to your body language; how you stand and sit also sends a message. Stand tall, head up, and feet a shoulder's width apart. If you're sitting, sit tall with both feet on the floor. Own your space. Just watch different people around the office or even at a party. You can see their level of confidence through their body language.

Be aware of the role you take in the conversation. According to Muriel James and Dorothy Jongeward in *Born to Win* (1978), we typically fall into one of three roles when speaking with others: the child, the adult, or the parent. The goal is to act as an adult, treating the other person with respect as an adult as well. Don't fall into the child role in answering to others, even when they have put themselves into the parent role (the parent role, in this context, is more of a condescending, "you answer to me" role). Respect yourself, and rise to the adult role.

Say yes to show your confidence—as long as you back it up. Entrepreneur Richard Branson claims that making a conscious decision to say yes to more things is one of his secrets for success. "Yes, I can do that. Is next month okay to start?" Set clear expectations with the *yes.*

Rather than "I can't," say, "How will I do this?" It shifts your mind to open up to the possibility that it can be done! "I can't get this project done by Monday" becomes "How can I get this project done by Monday?" It changes the way you think about it. It opens up possibilities and helps you feel more confident.

While confidence is necessary, there are times when we need to tone it down. We need to balance confidence with humility. For example, to show humility, we might want to share our vulnerabilities. As we talked about in Chapter 4, this builds trust. Giving someone else credit for something you both did can show you are humble and gives other people the chance to have the limelight. Balancing confidence with being humble creates an even stronger, more confident, and trustworthy image.

Inspire with Your Message

Good leaders inspire people to have confidence in their leader. Great leaders inspire people to have confidence in themselves.

—Eleanor Roosevelt

We can use our communication to inspire and move people. The right words, tone, and positive energy can get people up and dancing—or running, or working, or advocating! We can propel people into action with our message. Leaders must be able to inspire others to take action, and the way they inspire differs, depending on the person and the situation. Remember, be a chameleon, and communicate in the language of your people. Not everyone will be motivated by the same thing.

You can help shift people's thoughts and beliefs toward being more positive by asking reflective questions and using stories, analogies, quotes, and humor. Think of what you want to inspire them to do, and look for the appropriate venue. Is it a story, your own personal example, or maybe a fun analogy? Be authentic; make sure it comes from your heart. When it's too rehearsed, people may assume you're not genuine.

When you express gratitude, that, too, can inspire people. Not only will it help you feel happier and focus on the positive by expressing it but also it gives the other person a sense of meaning and purpose. Showing appreciation opens the door to abundance and generosity. Chapter 11 provides a step-by-step approach to recognition.

Just by keeping our words focused on the positive, we will be more inspiring. Saying, "Remember to . . ." is subtly more inspiring that saying, "Don't forget," which actually keeps us focused on what we're trying to avoid. *Remember* helps us focus on what we want. Review that list of words to avoid, and stay focused on words that inspire.

With awareness of your intent and mindfulness of your words and nonverbal communication, your message will come across as intended.

Is Sarcasm Your Scapegoat

Say what you mean, mean what you say and put a beat to it.

—Lewis Carroll, *Alice in Wonderland*

Sarcasm isn't always intended to be negative. It can be fun and a lighter way to approach a topic, but it can also be very damaging and demeaning. I've worked with organizations where sarcasm was used appropriately, and people understood and enjoyed it, and with other organizations where it has been abused and not useful.

It's all about the intent behind it and how a person receives it. Are you trying to get at someone or say something you're too uncomfortable to say outright? Or are you just having some fun and being witty and actually a bit affectionate with your sarcasm, like when you pick on someone because you really care about them, versus you pick on someone because you're just being mean? There's a difference in condescending, cocky messages and poke-fun-at-you well-intended messages. While your intent is very important, equally important is how a person perceives what you are saying.

When you hide behind sarcasm, what you say usually backfires. People either don't get it, or if they do they are so ticked off about the way you said it and the way it made them feel that they don't want to do anything you are asking. Especially as a formal leader in an organization, you have to have the courage to say what you need to say and not hide behind sarcasm.

Remember from Chapter 3 that emotions can be great triggers, if we pay attention. With empathy, you can be aware of another person's emotions. When you notice a reaction to something you've said, use it as a way to reflect on what you've said and if it was the right way to say it. As a receiver of a sarcastic message, have courage to speak up and let the other person know when the message is coming across as sarcastic and not helpful. You could do this more subtly by saying something like "I'm not sure what you're asking me to do."

The next time you feel like being sarcastic, just quickly reflect and ask yourself what your real intent is. Be brutally honest with yourself. If there's something you need to say and it's serious, then say it. Then joke around a bit if you want the person to feel better. But don't confuse the entire message by hiding behind the sarcasm.

The Illusion of Fear

The only thing we have to fear is fear itself.

—Franklin D. Roosevelt

As a child, I often heard fear-based messages: "Don't go out there alone or you might get stolen" or "Don't do that; you'll get hurt." Although well intended, these messages are creating fear. Self-esteem is built during childhood, and the messages we receive are the seeds of our esteem. All of those messages like "you can't" and "you'll never" make an impact. Some people might rebel and say, "Oh yes, I can," and they do it anyway. For others, they believe that they can't, and they make it a part of who they are.

Fear has been used as a means to control people from the beginning of time, and it continues in our politics, religions, schools, workplaces, and families. Some of it is intentional, but a lot of fear-based messages could be just habit or so deep-seated at a subconscious level that people are not aware. In the workplace, we communicate fear with threats and by focusing on the negative: "If we don't do this, our numbers will . . . " "You better do that or else." Even accountability is handled with fear, as we saw in Chapter 3.

The thing is that fear works—in the short term—because people have been conditioned with fear. The problem is that we don't see the undercurrent and what it is causing. We don't see the resistance and lack of productivity. We only see how people jump and react to our bullying and threats.

It's true, people need to respect consequences, but the energy behind it doesn't have to be fear-based. We can be realistic and tell it like it is. A leader should be building confidence and self-esteem, not instilling fear. Be clear on expectations and consequences, both positive and negative. Let people make the choice that will lead to whatever consequence they want.

Respect People's Time

Time is the most valuable thing a man can spend.

—Theophrastus

Many years ago, I learned a valuable lesson from a boss about respecting other people's time. I remember taking great pride in keeping my desk clean and having all my tasks completed promptly. Whenever anyone brought something in for my boss, I looked it over, put a Post-it note on it letting him know the gist of it, and brought it right into his office. I really thought I was doing a great job until one day he very calmly and clearly said to me, "It's great you are completing things and getting things to me so timely. You know what could help me even more? If you could consider whether I need the information you're bringing in right away, or if it could wait until the end of the day or even midday when I leave for lunch. Every time you come in, it interrupts what I am doing."

Wow, I hadn't even thought of it that way. The message I was probably sending to my boss without even realizing it was that my stuff was more important and/or I didn't respect his time. Considering other people's time sends the message that you care about the big picture, not just about yourself. Remember, actions speak louder than words.

Safe Communication—Use a Filter

Showing your personality doesn't mean you have to show everything.

—Marie Forleo

As we learned from Chapter 3, communicating with integrity doesn't mean we say everything on our minds. Some things may not be helpful for others to hear. When we respect that our perception may not be the other person's perception or reality, we decide what and how much is appropriate to share. Is there a good reason to bring it up, or is it our own issue? Just because you believe it to be true, do you need to share it?

When Bob told me he prided himself in being direct and telling it like it is, I knew he didn't realize that he blurted things out that weren't relevant and, quite frankly, came across as disrespectful. For example, he openly shared his opinions on what women in the office were wearing, and he shared things like this during client meetings. Consequently, he was being coached on this because he didn't see it as a problem. It was what he considered truth, so he felt he should say it. With some help, Bob learned he had to use filters—not blurt out anything he was thinking, no matter how true he believed it was.

Being honest doesn't mean putting everything out on the table. Respect the situation, and keep your message relevant. If there is a valid reason to bring something up, choose words that are helpful and not hurtful; for example, rather than using an irritated tone of voice and saying "What are you talking about?" you might say "I'm not sure if I'm seeing this the same way as you" or "I'm not sure if I understand this." Sift through your vocabulary to find the best words, so the other person has an opportunity to be open and they can understand.

Filters come in handy when you don't want to share certain information. Frankly, it may not be any of their business—not in a mean, patronizing fashion, but in a matter-of-fact, confident way. Or, it could be damaging to share certain information. We often feel compelled to share a lot more than we have to or should. Maybe it's the way we grew up, our parents and teachers demanded to know and we obeyed. As adults, there are many things that we may want to share, depending on the relationship, and many things we don't have to share or shouldn't share. When you are clear on what's important, it's much easier to decide what information is appropriate for your message.

In developing a training program for one of my manufacturing clients a few years back, I was working with the human resource manager, Julie. Julie was sharing with me how difficult it was to keep the secret of the layoffs from her friends. She felt like she was betraying them. When I had Julie consider the damage that sharing the information could cause, she accepted the reason but was still not feeling it was right. A few months later, that manufacturing facility received a very large contract, and the layoffs were canceled. This made Julie realize the value of confidentiality. Had people known, they most likely would have been negative, disengaged, and focused on finding new jobs, and productivity would have been affected. Who knows, with that distraction, that large contract may not have come in.

Structure Your Message

Either write something worth reading or do something worth writing.

—Ben Franklin

How can we expect people to listen and engage if they can't understand our message? We need to think of it from their point of view: Respect what other people need to know, how much, and by when. This sets the stage for more clarity and timeliness. Stop for a moment right now. Take a piece of paper, and fold it into a tent (so you can stand it up and see it on your desk). Now jot down: Who else needs to know, how much, by when? This reminder will help you provide information to people who need to be included and avoid sending it to people who don't. It will help you decide what they need to know and not include unnecessary details or leave out important ones. And it will help you be timely, keeping people in the loop but not interrupting them unnecessarily.

Rather than just shooting from the hip with what you need to say, are you thinking ahead about the best way to say it?

What exactly is your purpose? What main points do you need to get across, and what important information do they need? How do you want them thinking and feeling?

Take the time to structure your message, so people have the best opportunity to understand and retain it. Don't be human spam, a term I picked up in an article I read posted by Team Fascinate: "If no one gets value out of your communication, it's spam." When we share too much useless data or information, or when we're taking up too much time and space with what we are saying, our message isn't clear enough, and it can be annoying to others. You end up being placed in the category with all their other time thieves, and they may avoid listening to you in the future.

A simple way to stay focused on the important aspects to include in your message is QQT: quantity, quality, and timeliness. Expectations are clearer when we include quantity, quality, and timeliness in our message, and it is easier to help people stay on track, which we'll discuss further in Chapter 11. On the flip side, if you aren't getting enough details, think about asking for QQT.

Recognize DiSC® styles and the situation to help you structure your message. Here are a few tips for things to consider for each style:

- People with D behavior want you to save them time, and they're most concerned with the *what*. Begin with the punch line.
- People with i style like the highlights, they want you to save them effort, and they are concerned with the *who*, the people side of things.
- People with S style don't want conflict, are most concerned with *how* this is going to pan out in particular for everyone involved, and they want to hear about the process.
- People with C style want you to save them embarrassment, are most concerned with getting things done perfectly, and want

to make sure there is a good structure and plan to follow. They are most concerned with the *why*.

If we take the time to consider whom we are speaking to and the core message we want to get across, we can be mindful of the structure of our messages. It may take a bit of patience for some of us who just want to come out with it and get things rolling. But if we think about how to say it best, it will be accepted and implemented a lot more efficiently and effectively—whether it's one on one, formal or informal, in an e-mail or voicemail, in a meeting, or when you're speaking in public.

When you fail to structure your message, it can be perceived that you don't care enough to think it through, and that subtle message comes across to your team or your audience. At the very least, people are most likely missing your message.

Public Speaking: It's Not about You

The words of the songs, not the person, is what attracts people.

—Bob Marley

Public speaking has been said to be one of people's greatest fears of all, even more than death. What is it that scares the crap out of us? Is it not looking perfect, not being liked, being rejected, forgetting what we have to say and feeling stupid? For most of us, as comical as it might be, picturing the audience naked is not the answer! But it does help to realize that the answer is going to be different for each of us, because our fears and experiences are different. As has been the theme, we need to be aware and identify the truth of the situation. What is it that scares us? Stalk yourself before getting up to speak or when thinking about having to speak in public, ask yourself what is scaring you. What is the worst thing that could happen? Do some deep soul searching if necessary. Get a coach to help you figure it out.

For some of us, it is the fear of not being liked. In this case, be real and genuine. If you prepare your message and then speak from your heart, that's the best way you can connect with others, and they will like you. It helps to have a topic you enjoy, so if you don't get to pick your topic, find something that you enjoy about it.

I had a professor in college who took a very pragmatic approach to public speaking. One of the greatest lessons I learned from him was that it's really not about me. We worry too much about ourselves: how we look, how we sound, whether they like us. If we think of ourselves as simply a messenger and our goal is to help the audience, our intent changes. This allows us to connect with people and give them a gift. Talk about GRIT® and generosity!

Share Your Message with the World

The meaning of life is to find your gift. The purpose of life is to give it away.

—William Shakespeare

I believe we all have a message to share. Our message might be shared in a number of ways—by the work we do, with our words, or through our music or the art we create. I was working with my client Dave about his fear of performing. He has a gift of music, and his passion has motivated him to practice playing guitar faithfully. He's very good, but he's hesitant and nervous about playing in front of people. We talked for a bit to heighten his awareness of his thoughts and beliefs around this. He came around to see that if he loves playing so much, why not share that with others? It's a gift. And it's really not about him; he's a messenger. I joked with him and told him he's essentially obligated to share his gift with the world! Well, I may have been stretching it a little here, but the point is that people appreciate the gift. I shared how much I love the way live music makes me feel. It's motivational. It moves my soul. I'm so happy there are talented musicians to give us music. Dave said that when he thought about it this way, it wasn't so intimidating.

For any of us, what is our message to the world—what is our gift we have to give? Whether you're Joe Cross of *Fat, Sick and Nearly Dead*, helping people get healthy, or you're one of the George Carlins of the world, helping us laugh and lighten up—we all have a message. We all have a gift to share.

The next time you're nervous about sharing your message, remember that many people are really moved by my message, or your song, or her painting. It's something we can give to other people, and the message is love. Believe in yourself. What you have really is a gift for people. As a leader, you have a gift to share. Your message helps people find purpose and direction; it inspires people and helps them stay on track. It helps people feel connected to something greater than themselves.

Yes, even when we do our best to send the right messages, stuff will happen because we're dealing with an entire planet of other human beings who have their own idea of passions, priorities, and values—and their own ways of sending their messages. Mesh us all together, and there's bound to be some differences, especially when fear and other negative emotions get in the way. We also have a lot of similarities. Embrace both differences and similarities, don't take it so personally, and lighten up about it. Life is here for us all to live and be happy and share our message.

Your message is a reflection of who you are and what you stand for. When sending messages, keep these tips in mind:

- Know your purpose.
- Visualize the outcome, and keep the end in mind. How do you want people to feel and think? What do you want as a result of this message?

- Communicate the why, the what, and the how. Consider who else needs to know, how much, by when. Keep QQT in mind (quantity, quality, timeliness).
- Adapt your style to your listener.
- Ask questions, then LAF: listen, acknowledge, and follow up.
- And laugh—yes, enjoy the interaction and connections you make.

Before you venture into Chapter 9, take some time to reflect.

What SHIFT Will You Make?

Scan the chapter. List the topics that resonated with you.

_____

_____

Hone in on one or two areas that will make the biggest impact for you.

_____

_____

Imagine the impact. Why is this important? How will you feel when you've accomplished this?

_____

_____

Figure out your plan and how you will stay on track.

_____

_____

Take action. Start now. Schedule it now, and include your follow-up.

_____

_____

Enjoy! Remember to choose to be happy, every step of the way!

Reference

James, M., Jongeward, D. (1978). *Born to Win: Transactional analysis with gestalt experiments.* New York, New York: New American Library.

CHAPTER NINE

JUST SAY IT!

The single biggest problem in communication is the illusion that it has taken place.

—George Bernard Shaw

- Your boss keeps piling on the work while your coworker skates by with the minimum. You want to keep your job, so you keep your mouth shut.

- You work on a team, and another member of the team is chronically late with her piece of the puzzle. You are beyond frustrated, but you don't have the power or authority to do or say anything.

- Your coworker is constantly negative with you and positive in front of the boss. Knowing he can be positive with the boss, and he is choosing to be negative with you, infuriates you. You decide to give him a taste of his own medicine by being negative to him.

Whether it's saying no, standing up for yourself, pointing out something that needs to change, or even saying something positive, ironically, the things we need to say the most are the things we avoid saying. Or we wait until we're so frustrated or angry that we lash out with hurtful words or talk behind the person's back—damaging important relationships. Why does this happen?

There could be a number of reasons that we don't say what we need to. Sometimes we're afraid it will be taken the wrong way, or we just don't know how to say it. Often we want to avoid conflict altogether. Many of us don't want to open that can of worms.

If you are not willing to say what you want or need to say, use that as an awareness and trace your way through GRIT® to see what might be happening with you. What we tend to do is focus externally on the person or the situation, rather than internally on ourselves. Perhaps we're not respecting ourselves by getting the proper rest, food, and exercise we need, so we're tired and grumpy and don't have the energy to have the conversation. Or maybe we've become the White Knight, and while we're saving everyone else's day, we're depleting ourselves, burning out, and unable or unwilling to say what we need to say.

Say It to Help Others

Unless someone like you cares a whole awful lot, nothing is going to get better. It's not.

—Dr. Seuss

When we communicate with GRIT®, there is no avoidance, no hesitation, no effort. It's easy to say what you need to say. You have a positive intent, and you say it in a way that gives the person the best opportunity to be open to hearing it.

Remember The Five Steps of Change™ (see Figure 9.1)? You can use that to guide you with having these conversations.

The intent is to help someone with an awareness and inspire the person to want to make a change (the desire). You might support and encourage them by sharing some ideas of how to do it (the knowledge) and work out the steps it takes

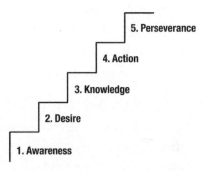

Figure 9.1. The Five Steps of Change™

to make it happen (action). You're there for them to help them stay on track (perseverance).

While being direct is important, the first thing out of your mouth might very well be the most important. You're setting the stage to help the other person be open to listen. In fact, it can be more damaging to say it wrong than to not say it at all! Reflect for a moment on your intent. Why are you having this conversation? Then consider how this particular person might best receive the message, which will help you select the right words.

Be mindful of the DiSC® styles we shared in the last chapter. Remember that we are a mix of DiSC® and that people are adjusting and adapting all the time, so be careful not to label a person with only one DiSC® style that never changes. In general, the following will help with how you can open the dialogue with each of the DiSC® styles.

- Ds don't want you to waste their time, so spit it out; don't sugarcoat it. Keep the tone matter-of-fact.

- Cs don't prefer a lot of fluff around it, either. They are most concerned with perfection and quality, so we don't want to sound like we're criticizing.
- Ss are typically the most sensitive, so our tone of voice and sharing our intent will be important.
- And the i is concerned with image and likes to keep things light, so keep it informal but still direct.

In addition to DiSC®, there are other things to consider, like confidence level, the trust and respect you have with each other, and personal issues that someone may be dealing with. Bear in mind that everyone isn't just like you, so respect that someone may need to hear a message differently than you would.

Although we can't control another person's reaction, we can certainly do our best to choose our words and tone. Depending on the situation, there are many different ways to open that conversation you're avoiding. Let's take a look at a few.

One of my favorites is to simply ask a question that helps a person with awareness: "Hey Joe, not sure if you realized the report was due today?" Stop for a moment and consider how important your tone of voice and your nonverbals will be. Remember to keep a positive intent, and it will come through.

At times it can be helpful to point to a common goal—obviously it has to be the other person's goal too: "I know we both want to finish this up on time." The other person will more open to hearing what else you have to say.

Sharing our intent can help the other person understand and be more receptive: "I really want to help find a win-win solution to this." Another example: "Hey, Joe, I'm telling you this because I care." Again, it has to be genuine, and you'd need a good foundation of trust for this one.

Staying neutral and taking *you* out of your language can help open the door: Rather than saying, "You promised to get me that information by today! You didn't keep your promise!" you can say, "This project requires everyone's commitment to the deadline—we won't be successful without your input."

If you've been clear on expectations or agreements you've made with someone, you can refer to that: "Okay, here's an example of what we were talking about—what not to do. . . ."

People often need to hear facts and details, so they can be clear on the issue. Explaining the impact of the situation can help a person understand why it's important. This information typically comes immediately after the opening statement and sometimes can actually be a part of your opening statement: "I know we both want to finish this up on time. Not sure if you realized I've got about 15 hours to put into it and will need a few days, so that's why I needed it from you yesterday." Giving the details and the impact helps the person relate and hopefully commit.

Allowing the other person a moment to explain or just let it sink in is important. We often rush right through without pausing. Most of us aren't comfortable with silence. Think of silence as that person's opportunity to commit to a change. Sure, sometimes they are going to need more encouragement or more reasons. And sometimes we'll need to escalate to the next level. Say Joe just doesn't care about your deadline. The next conversation might go something like this: "Well, Joe, I can appreciate you're busy, too. We made a promise to Jacqueline that this would be finalized by Friday. If we can't figure it out together, let's go talk to her." If he refuses, you simply let him know you will be going to talk to her.

Personal situations can often be more difficult because you're emotionally attached. But if you really care about someone, and that person is open to hearing feedback, then tell the truth. For example, perhaps you notice something that you think would be helpful for your friend to know. Let's say it's about something she's wearing—she's looking heavy in the outfit she just put on. Do you tell her? Obviously the way you say it depends on your situation, but here are a few examples. If in the past she invited you or instructed you to tell her of any such situations, then yes, you tell her, gently. For example, "Remember when you told me that you would want to know if your jeans looked too tight?" or another way might be "Hey, you had told me a while back you always want me to be honest with you. Do you feel like hearing something now?" Always consider timing: Will it tear down confidence? How can it be done in the right way so it doesn't?

When you're faced with a really tough conversation, you might take the time to draft what you're thinking and feeling first. Then put it into a deliverable statement. Terminating someone is a good example. Often we feel guilty or sympathetic to the person. If we are aware of our thoughts and feelings first, it will help bring clarity to why we might be avoiding it and how we can say it with integrity and respect. After all, if we've given the person the opportunity to succeed, it's really up to him to decide if he wants to.

We not only avoid conversations in which we want someone to change, but we also avoid conversations that recognize people for doing things right or just show our appreciation. Did you ever notice when you have something nice to say about someone, you typically tell someone else about that person, rather than saying it directly to them? Sure, it's nice to let other people know, but we're missing a great opportunity to say it directly to the person. You can do both. Chapter 11 provides specific GRIT® steps for delivering positive and constructive feedback in the workplace.

With GRIT®, you'll genuinely want to have these conversations because your intent is to help. Generosity comes naturally, as you want to give others an opportunity for awareness. They can then decide to change, or not, and you will respect their choice.

Make Waves

Difficulties are meant to rouse, not discourage. The human spirit is to grow strong by conflict.

—William Ellery Channing

People are not always going to agree. For many, these disagreements can be uncomfortable. We want everyone to get along and be happy and make no waves, as if waves are not good. Waves don't need to be scary—they can be enjoyable, of course, with respect for them—just ask any surfer!

The way we think about conflict and our beliefs around it can prevent us from dealing effectively with it. Think about the importance of conflict. We need healthy debate to get ideas on the table, to consider things that could get in the way of our success, to show respect for opposing opinions, and to air it all out, so we can move forward. If we keep things in, it will come out in other ways.

Our thoughts and beliefs about conflict are often shaped in childhood and can be etched into our brains. In theory, we all know that yelling and screaming gets us nowhere, but then we find ourselves caught up in the moment, and our negative emotions and ego have taken over. We can change the way we deal with conflict. But we must respect the fact that each of us has past experiences with handling conflict, and it takes time to make new habits. All the work we've done in Part I with GRIT® enables us to gracefully handle the waves of conflict. With the right environment of trust and respect, we can change the way people deal with conflict. And just imagine, like the surfer with the waves, you can use this dialogue to carry you forward, rather than never getting in and enjoying the water!

Consider these tips for engaging in healthy dialogue:

- Be aware of your own intent, and make sure you're being objective.
- Be mindful of what you are focusing on; don't get sucked into something.
- Get individual ego out of the way (feeling more than or less than).
- Meet conflict head-on. Bring attention to it, rather than ignoring it and hoping it just goes away.
- Plan for and communicate frequently and openly.
- Be honest about concerns; share your intent.
- Communicate honestly and avoid playing gotcha-type games. (There's that ego again!)
- Agree to disagree: Understand healthy disagreement will build better decisions. (Be aware of why you avoid disagreement. What are you concerned about?)
- Discuss differences openly.
- Get your team involved; people will support what they help create.
- Provide more data and information than is needed.
- Use helpful language:
  - You're right. I see how you feel about that.
  - Can you consider this perspective?
  - May I share how I feel?

Empower Team Communication

Individual commitment to a group effort—that is what makes a team work, a company work, a society work, a civilization work.

—Vince Lombardi

Consider the value of healthy dialogue to the success of a team. If team members cannot talk directly to each other, guess who's fixing all the problems? You. The leader. More often than not, a manager steps in to fix the problem, rather than empower the team to communicate directly and figure things out. This creates more problems and a long line outside your door. If you want to shorten that line, get your people talking directly to each other. Empower them to solve problems with each other. For example, the next time someone comes into your office with a problem, ask questions rather than solve it. You could start by asking them to clearly define the problem (in as few words as possible). Then, ask them what they can do about it. Keep the ownership with them. Remember the Accountability Ladder from Chapter 3—you want them to take ownership and make it happen. So last, ask them if they really needed to see you about it. Coach people to think this way, and you'll notice the line at your door drastically decreases.

When you listen to every problem and solve it for people, especially when it's something that involves another person, it could actually be promoting gossip. Gossip is toxic to an organization. It erodes trust and respect. It is a huge waste of time. We should be stepping in only when the communication between two people has broken down, and then we only need to be helping them communicate—not solving the problem for them. If you make a regular practice of forcing the conversation and not fixing their problems, you'll spend less time coaching and counseling them to fix things later.

Then there are those triangulated conversations—the he said, she said talk going on that was mentioned in Chapter 4. We've all been caught up in it. You know how it goes: Joe approaches you to complain about an issue he is having with John, rather than addressing the issue directly with John. Sure, sometimes we need to vent and maybe get someone to help us with how we need to address something, but all too often people are engaging in triangulated conversations, and they have no intention of going directly to the person. They just want to complain.

As the receiver of this information, it's pretty important how you respond to it. There are different ways depending on the situation, but the bottom line is that we have to help Joe see that if he wants any kind of change, the only option is to talk directly with John. And all the excuses as to why not—they won't listen anyway, they aren't open to hearing it, they will just deny it, they won't see it the way I'm seeing it—can be handled face-to-face.

Feel, felt, found is one way to address this. Say to Joe: "Oh yeah, I know how you feel. It's so frustrating when people don't come through. I felt that way, too, in the past. You know what I found? Having a heart-to-heart very direct talk really helped the situation." Pause for Joe to respond or to just reflect a moment.

Continue by sharing with Joe, "Here's what I said when I was in a similar situation: 'Hey, Sue, can we talk about our project time lines? I know how busy you are and it's tough to get things to me on time. What can I do to help you make your deadlines?' Don't think I didn't feel like saying 'Every time you're late, it makes me late, and I'm scrambling to get things done. It's really frustrating, and it needs to stop. Can you please get your piece to me on time from now on?'

"You know, Joe, awareness has helped me realize that saying it that way doesn't help the person look for a new solution. It just accentuates what's wrong. Think about a positive solution and how you can help, and the conversation goes a whole lot better than if you're so frustrated that you can hardly even approach the person."

Helping Joe to see that you've been there, you get it, and it can work out okay will give him the confidence to have the conversation. It can also be helpful to show an example of how a triangulated conversation can backfire or be useless, so he can see why it's so important for him to have the conversation directly with John.

Of course, if Joe hasn't built any kind of trust with John, it makes it much more difficult to have a meaningful conversation. With GRIT®, we've respected other people and taken the time to build relationships and trust. Even if we don't like someone, we can respect that the person is a member of the team and an important piece of the puzzle, so communication and trust are paramount.

When people refuse to have the conversation, we need to let them know that if they won't talk about it, here and now, then we'll have to get our manager involved to help. The manager will be helping the two people communicate—not fixing their problems. And when the manager taps John on the shoulder to talk, John will know he's not getting accused of what Joe said, but he's getting talked to about refusing to have the conversation. Managers need to encourage and enforce direct conversations among the team.

Just Say NO!

Have the courage to say no. Have the courage to face the truth. Do the right thing because it is right. These are the magic keys to living your life with integrity.

—W. Clement Stone

Saying no can be challenging for many people, with certain situations more challenging than others. For some of us, we can't say no at work, whether it's to a boss, a peer, or a direct report. For others, it's saying no in our personal lives that's more difficult—to a parent, a child, a friend, a lover.

Why is it so difficult to say no? Sometimes finding the why might help us with having the courage to say no. When we consider that the need to feel connected to others is one of the top needs of human beings, it's no wonder we avoid saying no. The problem is we're making a false assumption—that if we say no, they won't like us, they won't keep us around, or they will reject us in some way.

With GRIT®, we know what's important to us, and we know what we have to do to stay aligned. We have confidence and courage. We respect ourselves enough to keep focused on what's important, while respecting the needs of others. We don't give too much of ourselves, because that will end up depleting us. If we keep mindful of this, it will be easier to say no when you need to. Then we can use GRIT® as our guide to confidently say no, in a way that isn't fearful or mean.

Start by considering the truth of the situation and what you need to say, and then phrase it in a respectful way. And be generous, don't keep it to yourself—say it! Keep these important points in mind when you're saying no:

- Staying true to yourself and your goals is critical, and in the long run, you aren't helping anyone by straying.

- Be realistic with your time—it's a precious commodity. Choose where you want to spend it. It's up to you and no one else.

- Listen fully to the request. Don't get caught making assumptions before the person is finished speaking.

- Respect the other person's situation. Consider how you can say no in the best way, yet still directly.

- Don't feel obligated to explain. You have a right to stay aligned to your priorities and do what is best for you.

- If you do wish to explain, keep it simple and focused on the positive.

- Stand firm. Don't give in to their emotional cries.

- Be generous in the right way—if you give too much and then you can't deliver, you're really not in integrity or respecting yourself.

- It's your time. It's your choice. It's your responsibility.

Let's look at how we might say no in a few examples:

- As a member of the administrative support team, I have three bosses I report to. They all bring in top priority work that needs to be done yesterday! I can't say no to any of them because it's my job to support them.

Reply: "I want to make sure I'm working in the priority order that's best for the department. Can you help me see where your project fits in?"

- I find myself always saying yes to my friends. I don't want to let them down. I end up not having enough time for myself, or I cancel so much on them it has become a joke.

Reply: "Okay, Samantha, I can only tell you maybe on this. I don't want to say yes and end up canceling." Or "As much as I'd love to say yes, I've got a lot on my plate right now, thanks."

- When you're out with your friends or clients, and they want you to stay for another drink. "Oh come on, just one more!"

Reply: "Hey, I like to have fun as much as the next person, but I know my limits, and I want to feel good for (xyz) tomorrow."

- To clients who want more services but not be charged. "Hey, can you throw that in, too?"

Reply: "Sure, it's only $150 more to include that. Do you want to do that?" Or if you don't know the price: "Sure, I'll let you know how much that is."

We can say no without using the word *no*. Think positively about how you can help, without sacrificing yourself.

Just Ask

Take the attitude of a student, never be too big to ask questions, never know too much to learn something new.

—Og Mandino

Have you ever found yourself hedging on a question, only to find that the answer was not what you had dreaded? It's easy to do. We build up this story in our mind, often without awareness that we're doing it. We sense something is wrong in the relationship, but we just don't want to ask the question for fear of what we might hear. Even if it's just to avoid the conflict, we avert the question. We'll go on talking about anything else, pretending everything is okay; meanwhile, the elephant in the room is growing bigger!

Why don't we just ask the question? Often we go on our merry way with our own thoughts rather than stopping and asking the question. Well, sometimes we're not so merry about it; we might actually be suffering. What prevents us from asking more questions?

We may have been conditioned in our past to refrain from asking questions, maybe in childhood at school or at home. It's not uncommon for some people to want control and keep you from asking questions. Or a person doesn't want to take the time to think about the question and have to answer, so they steer you into not asking questions. It could be we're afraid of what the answer will be, so we don't even want to ask the question. Somewhere along the way, we may have learned that it's not a good thing to ask questions, and then it becomes habitual to not ask questions. If we don't ask, how will we know?

Perhaps a client or executive is talking about something so confidently and smoothly that you feel you should know what they are talking about. You've been bruised in your past by asking a question, only to be laughed at for not knowing an actor's name or some other trivial detail. It's better to admit that you don't know what they are talking about, rather than go on as if you know. Just lightly say, "Maybe I should know this, but I have to ask, who is that?"

When your intuition is telling you it's not a good fit, be it a prospect or romantic partner, you might refrain from asking the question because you're not really sure how to say it. Or maybe a part of you doesn't want to know. To keep going as if nothing's wrong will not fix any potential problems. It's better to get it out on the table. "I want to make sure we're on the same page, and I'm wondering what your expectations are for this relationship?"

Another reason we don't ask questions is that we don't want to stop the flow of the conversation and waste time. Rather than avoid asking, simply say "I have one quick question before we continue."

All of the reasons we don't ask questions have something in common. When you think about each of the examples, what is the common theme? Yes, it's that four-letter F word again—fear. There's some kind of fear that is stopping us from asking. The fears could be "I'm not smart enough," "I'm not good enough," "I'm not going to have enough time"—to name just a few. Remember, fear can help us recognize something about ourselves, if we choose to use awareness to shed light on it. We may need to change our thoughts and beliefs. Use Part I to refresh when you're hesitating to ask a question.

If we are being authentically generous, we will ask questions. We can be positive and respectful; we can share our intent. Have the courage to ask. Be respectful that the answer may not be what you were looking for. Each person has the right to their own answer. It's nothing personal. They have the right to stay true to themselves.

Use this three-step template to help you prepare for difficult conversations, and refer to Chapter 11 for specific GRIT® steps for constructive and reinforcing feedback.

1. What is my intent? Why am I having this conversation? (If it's not to help in some way, you may want to reconsider.)
2. What do I need to say? No edits—just jot it down.
3. How can I say it best, considering everything I know about the person and situation (DiSC® style, confidence level, timing)?

As with all leadership best practices and similar to parenting, practice and perseverance are key. We have to stay the course, keep asking questions and saying what we need to say, so it becomes an expectation. If a person or child knows they can beat you down, they will. We are responsible for setting the boundaries. If you stay strong and true, people will respect that, and you won't experience as much resistance. With GRIT®, it is much easier and more efficient and effective to say what you need to say, and you'll be setting the example, so others will do the same.

Before you venture into Chapter 10, take some time to reflect.

What SHIFT Will You Make?

Scan the chapter. List the topics that resonated with you.

_____

_____

Hone in on one or two areas that will make the biggest impact for you.

_____

_____

Imagine the impact. Why is this important? How will you feel when you've accomplished this?

_____

_____

Figure out your plan and how you will stay on track.

_____

_____

Take action. Start now. Schedule it now, and include your follow-up.

_____

_____

Enjoy! Remember to choose to be happy, every step of the way!

_____

_____

PART III

YOUR IMPACT

We've spent the first two sections of the book focused on the foundation of GRIT® and how we use GRIT® to communicate more effectively. Now let's take a look at how you impact others in your role as a leader, how to keep people on track, and what it takes to enjoy the journey.

CHAPTER TEN

THE RIPPLE EFFECT

Ripples

Raindrops
Touch
The Surface
Of a Pond

There Is
Movement

Then Ripples

This Is
How It Works

© 2007 Raymond Justice

Jane couldn't believe the e-mail she just received from the CEO—copying the entire management team. The language was demeaning and disrespectful, reprimanding her for something when he wasn't fully aware of the details. Sure, he was probably frustrated walking into the project expecting it to be complete, but what the CEO wrote was something you would

say if you were venting to a trusted friend over a
couple of drinks where no one would ever hear you.
Not only did he cut her down, but he bashed half of
her staff as well. It didn't take long for it to leak,
spreading to the rest of the organization. It would be
difficult to truly calculate the amount of time wasted
gossiping over this, the loss of potential sales, and the
missed opportunities for creativity.

Most people realize that negative behavior can be lethal,
spreading toxins throughout an organization. And when
it's the boss or someone else with authority, the impact can
be even more toxic because of this person's power and reach.
The ripple effect of how this event was handled will continue to have negative repercussions for weeks and months
to come.

When we feel we have no
control over circumstances, it
can be easy for us to then use
those circumstances as an excuse
to blame and complain and
even become stuck, waiting for
something to change. Think of
the Accountability Ladder from
Chapter 3 (see Figure 10.1). If we
realize this is the reality of the
situation, and then we consider
how we can make an impact, we
will shift to feeling that we can
make a difference. Sure, maybe

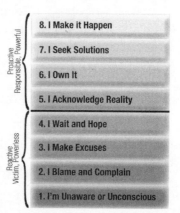

Figure 10.1. The Accountability Ladder

we don't own the company, or we feel like we don't have a
high enough position to make changes, but we can still have
an impact. It's been frequently reported that people don't leave

companies; people leave their managers. As a manager, you have a direct influence on your team, and you can make a difference.

Leaders set the stage. We are responsible for creating the culture that people are attracted to and feel committed to being a part of. Business Dictionary defines *culture* as "the values and behaviors that contribute to the unique social and psychological environment of an organization. It is based on shared attitudes, beliefs, customs and written and unwritten rules that have been developed over time and are considered valid." Changing culture is about getting individuals to change their behavior. Whether written as a mission statement, spoken, or merely understood, corporate culture describes and governs the way a company's owners and employees think, feel, and act.

A culture with GRIT® is where people step up, make things happen, take personal accountability, help each other to succeed, and are collectively focused on the greater goal. The members of your team support your ripple, rather than make their own splashes.

Your Ripple

Alone we can do so little; together we can do so much.

—Helen Keller

As a formal or informal leader in your organization, you influence people around you. A formal leader has the obligation and responsibility to do this. A formal leader not only has responsibility for himself but also is now responsible for the success of his team. Taking the focus off ourselves and putting it onto our people, without sacrificing our own needs, can be difficult. It's moving from what we term an individual contributor to a leader, and it requires focusing on the greater vision and each team member, while staying true to oneself. A formal leadership role requires both functions of leading and managing and the ability to adapt appropriately to situations.

An informal leader doesn't hold a position of formal authority, but peers are choosing to follow her lead. As defined in www.BusinessDictionary.com, an informal leader is an "individual within an organization that is viewed as someone worth listening to due to their perceived experience and reputation among peers." Most likely this person is thinking of the team and adapting appropriately as well.

The question is, whether you're a formal or informal leader, what influence will you have? Will you choose to make a positive impact and spread generosity, respect, integrity, and truth, in spite of all the challenges you face? Even when the odds are stacked against you, do you have the courage and strength to stay true to yourself? That's leading with GRIT®. You are being called to a higher level of leadership performance that will have the greatest impact on your organization, as well as your own success and happiness in life.

What makes some companies so great to work for? Sure, it's the vision and the service or product, but it's more about what's behind that. It's the people and the positive ripple effect they make. These people have heart. They are connected! It's intentional leadership that is keeping people connected, through generosity, respect, integrity, and truth. I've had the pleasure of working with companies like this, and you can feel it almost instantly by the energy of the people.

A company that is in integrity has employees in the right positions who are working together in the same direction, efficiently and effectively reaching the company's vision, while meeting the needs of its employees. Their values are aligned, they are doing what they love to do, and they're making a good profit as a result.

Whether you know football or not, you probably know the name Joe Montana. He might be better known than our presidents! The famous quarterback for the San Francisco 49ers, Joe Cool, was a great example of a guy with vision, confidence, and fearlessness. He seemed to always have faith in himself and in leading his team to victory. His ability to bring a team back from what looked like defeat became known as Montana Magic. Montana appeared to have no doubt, no fear—just an unwavering desire to win and a belief in himself and his team. The ripple effect of his faith and conviction inspired his teammates to believe in success.

While relentlessly going toward that vision, we must balance it with respect and appreciation for people. Believe in your people. Your ability to visualize them as successful will accelerate their success and yours.

The intentional leader is setting a vision and creating goals that allow people to stretch and grow. The goals are purposefully just beyond their reach—not too far so they give up, but not too attainable, so the goal still creates a challenge to strive toward.

It Starts with You

You can't be what you can't see.

—Marian Wright Edelman

By starting with yourself, you demonstrate how positive and productive you are. It's infectious—people start to follow. That's why it's so important to begin with ourselves, as we did in Part I. Knowing our truth, making any changes we desire, and walking the talk are all critical to being able to influence others. You've got to believe in yourself. You've got to see yourself as a leader.

Be clear on your values, so others relate to you and respect you. Your values are what you stand for and what guide you to make decisions to stay in integrity. People need to know who you are, what you believe in, and that you believe in them, and they need to trust that you walk your talk. When you do, they will respect you. If you haven't done so already, take some time to reflect and articulate your values before moving on. Go back to Part I to help if you're feeling stuck in any way. This is your truth, and it is the core of your success.

The Value of Connecting

People will forget what you said, people will even forget what you did; people will never forget how you made them feel.

—Maya Angelou

As a leader, spending time communicating with people is paramount to their buying in and carrying out the vision. It's how people are going to get to know you, trust you, and respect you. Connect with them. Ask questions. It shows you care, and you get to learn about the team. Listen, actively and empathically as in Chapter 7. And remember to LAF (listen, acknowledge, and follow through) with your team. Find out about their passions, what motivates them, what they aspire to be and do, their fears, assumptions, and challenges. When we connect in this way, we build trust. Remember, people *want* to follow someone they trust.

Recognizing that everyone plays an important role helps people feel connected and inspired to do their best. There's a great story about Charles Plumb, a U.S. Navy jet pilot in Vietnam. After 75 combat missions, his plane was destroyed by a surface-to-air missile. Plumb ejected and parachuted into enemy hands. He was captured and spent six years in a communist

Vietnamese prison. He survived the ordeal and now lectures on the lessons learned from that experience.

One day, when Plumb and his wife were sitting in a restaurant, a man at another table came up and said, "You're Plumb! You flew jet fighters in Vietnam from the aircraft carrier *Kitty Hawk*. You were shot down!"

"How in the world did you know that?" asked Plumb.

"I packed your parachute," the man replied. Plumb gasped in surprise and gratitude. The man pumped his hand and said, "I guess it worked!"

Plumb assured him, "It sure did. If your chute hadn't worked, I wouldn't be here today."

Plumb couldn't sleep that night, thinking about that man. Plumb says, "I kept wondering what he had looked like in a Navy uniform: a white hat, a bib in the back, and bell-bottom trousers. I wondered how many times I might have seen him and not even said 'Good morning, how are you?' or anything because, you see, I was a fighter pilot and he was just a sailor." Plumb thought of the many hours the sailor had spent at a long wooden table in the bowels of the ship, carefully weaving the shrouds and folding the silks of each chute, holding in his hands each time the fate of someone he didn't know.

When you feel valued and connected, you feel respected. How do we show the people around us that we value and respect them, from our customers, to our employees, to our bosses, to our wives, our husbands, our parents, and our children?

Communication is what carries our message and keeps us connected—the ripple. As leaders we must be clear and organized so people have the best opportunity to understand and keep the message going. Some of us would prefer to just shoot from the hip. I have to admit that's my natural tendency, and it's rooted in my D/i behavioral style. But I know it takes discipline and time to think things through and structure the message so people get it. We've got to think about how they need to digest it, and we need to help them understand the why behind what we are doing. We can't just jump in with "This is what we're doing; now go do it!" For people to buy in, they need to understand the purpose and see how they are connected and meaningful to the vision or goal.

Leaders need to be able to have a high-quality dialogue to connect with their employees. Be open and respect employees' questions, their concerns, and their needs without judgment. For example, have a conversation with each direct report about how they want to be managed. Just to acknowledge that we hear them goes a long way with most people. Whether you can implement their request or not, if you're clear and honest with your decision, it will be respected. If we don't have conversations with our people, and if they don't trust that they can be open and honest, we won't know about potential problems. They can be like land mines—you hit one when you least expect it.

While many people think a leader's job is to control other people's behavior, it's not! It's to help people recognize and want to change their own behavior. A big part of leadership is influencing, and that includes being able to inspire people. It's important to remember that everyone is different and therefore inspired differently. It's not all rah-rah cheerleading that gets everyone fired up. Actually, that can demotivate a lot of people, especially if it's not genuine.

Be optimistic. You'll be more energetic, and you'll attract more optimistic people. An optimistic person tends to get more done in less time than a negative person. As we discovered in Part I, with GRIT® it's effortless. You are genuinely and naturally optimistic. If you're not feeling this way, reread Part I and see where you need to focus your efforts.

However you provide inspiration, be authentic, and then adjust to communicate in their language. For example, if you're extremely passionate and rah-rah, but your team is more reserved, you can still show your passion in a way that helps them connect. It's not just in the way you feel like showing it; it's in the way they will respect it. Remember, one of the biggest challenges as a leader might be to balance your own needs with the greater good of the team.

When you believe in your people and their potential, it's easier to visualize their success. You will look for the positive and encourage them. As Ben Herbster said, "The greatest waste in the world is the difference between what we are and what we could become." If you are frustrated and can't see their potential or visualize their success, you will look for the negative and discourage them. It goes back to what we discussed in Chapter 3: What you focus on, you will create more of.

When we believe in people and we give authentically to their development, we build trust and create an efficiency and effectiveness that's hard to beat. When we look at what we can put into people, rather than what we can get out of them, the energy completely changes. Employees are no longer adversaries—they become allies.

Think for a moment of someone you've worked for, a person who coached you on a team, or maybe a parent or teacher—someone in a leadership position whom you completely trusted. You felt they genuinely cared about you. How much more motivated were you to work for that person? I'll bet that when you think of the quality of your work, you didn't want to disappoint, so you strived to do your best. You cared about more than just yourself. This is another prime example of the law of giving and receiving, as we experienced in Chapter 5.

People may not notice or even appreciate the value of many of these things you do as a leader. Walking-around talking, connecting, and getting to know your people might not look like you're doing much. In fact, some people will view those activities as wasting time. Preventative measures or behind-the-scenes activities, like picking up trash or cleaning your house—people only notice when you haven't done them. As Benjamin Franklin said, "When the well's dry, we know the worth of water." It's one of those things that if you don't do it, it will have negative repercussions, but it's not always appreciated. Regardless, you can be sure that these preventive functions will create trust and loyalty that fuels more productivity, efficiency, and quality.

Spending the time to connect with your people and getting them to connect with each other might well be the best invest-ment you make as a leader.

Learn from the Chameleon

The wise adapt themselves to circumstances, as water molds itself to the pitcher.

—Chinese Proverb

Although we have many similarities, we do have our differ-ences. We learned in Chapter 4 the importance of respecting those differences. In a leadership role, it's even more critical. We have to know and respect our people. Spending time with each of them to get to know them is one way we already mentioned. We also have been talking about the value of the DiSC® assess-ment as a basis for understanding and appreciating similarities and differences in people. For leaders, it helps us with our own self-awareness of our natural tendencies and how we may need to adapt to be more successful with our people. If you haven't had the opportunity to explore DiSC® with your team yet, it is a safe and enjoyable way for your team to understand and appreciate each other, and it is very effective in helping people connect.

When I started working with a professional service firm out west we'll call ProServe, I learned very quickly that the behavior of one of the partners was causing most of the problems. The trick was to get this partner, Bill, to see it and believe if he changed, he would meet his goals faster, and overall the firm would be much healthier.

Bill drove people very hard. People complained of how arro-gant and condescending he was. Many examples of his rude and obnoxious behavior surfaced during interviews. I didn't have to press people for details—they needed to vent!

Ironically, he was also one of the most fun guys outside of work. Most people loved to have a beer with him! He was sociable and went to all of ProServe's functions. But this wasn't enough to keep people productive and inspired back at the office.

During our first meeting, to my surprise, Bill laid it all out on the table. He was aware of his behavior. Exactly how it was affecting the team, he was not so aware. He shared a lot with me that day. He was raised by a father who communicated with fear: command and control. It kept order in their household, and in Bill's view, it worked.

The message Bill adopted from his childhood was 'my way or the highway.' So he did what he knew best, what he had seen work. His intent was in the right place: He wanted people to be successful. He thought being friendly outside of the workplace would be enough. People would realize that at work he has to drive people hard to get results. What he didn't realize was that just because it was effective for him, his way of doing things would not work for everyone. In fact, it was actually undermining others' confidence and motivation. What he failed to recognize was that for a few people, his method might work; for most others, it will backfire and create issues—other issues that get in the way of reaching the goals, and it is much harder to pinpoint the cause of these issues. He wasn't aware of the negative ripple effect he was having on the team.

As evident by this case, although intent is very important and foundational, equally important is the message we deliver. Ownership of the way we communicate—what other people experience—is crucial to leadership success. We can't just think good things or be nice after work and a hard-ass on the job. We have to deliver a congruent message for people to trust and follow us. We have to talk in the language of our people.

Know the Skills You Need

Think like a wise man but communicate in the language of the people.

—William Butler Yeats

In leadership, as in life, there are different behaviors required for various situations. We've got to be able to size things up and adapt accordingly. It's like wearing the right clothes to each event—you wouldn't wear shorts and a tank top to the corporate business networking event!

Unlike the chameleon, one of the biggest mistakes managers make is not adjusting their management style to fit the situation. Most managers have a management style they are comfortable with, and that's what they use in almost every situation. But different situations call for different measures, and once a manager understands the benefits of making those adjustments, productivity increases and stress decreases.

It's not that difficult to adjust and adapt—if we're aware, and if we want to. Yes, it always starts with awareness. Take a look at your natural tendencies as a leader and where you might need to focus more energy at times to be a more effective leader. Our main purpose as leaders is to help people accomplish a goal or achieve a vision, to grow and develop, and to enjoy the journey. Throughout this process, a variety of skills are needed to engage people and make it a success. Some of those skills come naturally, and others need work. How do we know which ones need more attention?

The skill set it takes to lead a team is different from what it takes to be on a team or to be an individual contributor. Most of us were promoted without our boss realizing this, and without training in these skills. We need the right tools for any job. Professional assessments can help you become aware of your own strengths and limitations, and create a ripple to the rest of the team, so everyone has a common language, respect, and an understanding of each other.

There are many tools on the market today that can help us fine-tune our skills. DiSC® has been mentioned. There's also a leadership self-assessment I recommend that helps you discover your natural leadership tendencies and where you might need to focus more energy. It gives insight on how our tendencies impact our effectiveness in specific leadership situations. The report you receive as a result of your self-assessment concentrates on developing preferred behaviors that are based on best practices to help you become a more effective leader. The Work of Leaders® tool is one of the best leadership self-assessments I've ever used.

Building the Team

Coming together is a beginning. Keeping together is progress. Working together is success.

—Henry Ford

To carry out the vision and goals, we need the right team. An understanding and respect for people's similarities and differences will help you build that team. Without the right team, a leader is wasting time on unnecessary coaching, counseling, and disciplinary activities. We'll always need to coach and counsel, but we can alleviate a lot by getting the right people in place, based on the skills needed to reach the vision or goal.

It's not just about DiSC® and our leadership tendencies. We also need to look at the attitudes and beliefs people have, because as we know, thoughts and beliefs drive action. Working on changing someone's actions rather than their thoughts and beliefs is like expecting weeds not to grow back when you neglect to pull the roots.

Most of us don't get the
luxury of hiring a whole new
team, and even if we did, we
know there would still be human
dynamics we'll need to work
on. Helping our teams navigate
through change is one of them.
Not everyone is going to be a
change agent. So how do we
make change less painful and
more enjoyable? As you become

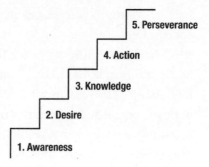

Figure 10.2. The Five Steps of Change™

familiar with The Five Steps of Change™, share it with your
teams (Figure 10.2). Help them to understand change, especially
that often change begins with our own thoughts and beliefs.

Remember it always starts with us, from the way we passion-
ately look at the goal to our eagerness to help someone develop
and grow; from the way they feel that we care about them to
the humor we bring to situations. We can change the way our
teams accept and promote change! We can make an impact on
the ripple of change.

Start by rallying those people on your team who are willing to
participate with you. They will help make your ripple bigger so any
other splashes being made won't interfere. Of course, we want to
prevent as many splashes as we can so our ripple spreads faster and
more efficiently. Look for those who might resist the change, and
be aware that some will be covert; they will be stirring things up
from below the surface, causing other people to kick and splash.
Look for opportunities to get them involved or get them out.

Nobody Wins Unless You Delegate

You only lose what you cling to.

—Buddha

Once we have the team in place and we've mitigated the splashes, it's time to get stuff done. Delegation allows our ripple to continue. Most of us would agree that we'd like to be able to delegate and trust that the job gets done right and on time. The biggest reason our expectation is not met when we delegate is typically that leaders have not considered if the person is able and willing to perform the task, and they delegate before employees are ready. There are other reasons we'll look at, too, but let's start here.

A person needs to be willing and able before delegation is effective. Can the person do it, and will the person do it? The first, ability, is knowing if they have the required skill set and experience. The second, willingness, can consist of attitude or confidence. People may lack confidence in a task, which can cause them to be unsure or unwilling to participate. Or a person's attitude can get in the way. Either way, it's not about the skill that it takes; it's the willingness that's missing. Both can have a negative impact on our ripple.

When we clearly understand these two components, we can adjust our management style to one that will produce results. For example, when a person's ability is low and their willingness is high, they are eager to be trained or directed on what to do. It's the manager's job to make sure they have this opportunity. At the same time, it's the manager's responsibility to decide if the employee is not capable, if there is another seat on the bus, or if that person needs another bus altogether.

When a person's ability is lower and/or their willingness is lower, they need coaching or guiding. If it's too low, they may need that other seat—on or off the bus. As their willingness and ability increase, all they need is your support. And finally, when their willingness and ability are high, they are ready for delegation. If we want our ripple to continue, we have to free up more of our time. Empowering people moves them to the delegation stage even faster. A chameleon changes to match the environment to survive. Think of your survival—learn to adjust to each situation.

There are other reasons that leaders are not effective with delegation. The top five reasons that I've experienced in organizations are as follows:

1. Not clear with expectations
2. Hasn't built relationships and trust
3. Isn't approachable or available
4. Doesn't set up the right checkpoints
5. Abdicates all responsibility

When we're leading with GRIT®, it's easier to delegate and step out of the way.

Attitude Is Everything

Attitude is a little thing that makes a big difference.

— Winston Churchill

Positive attitude is necessary on any team. You might have the most technologically skilled person, but her poor attitude affects the rest of the team and grossly outweighs the benefits of technical skills. These people are making the biggest splashes, or undercurrents, and are the toxins that will kill your project, wipe out your budget, or crush everyone else's creativity and passion.

There's a famous story about a traveler centuries ago who was walking across what is today France. This traveler came to an open area where hundreds of workers were busy laboring in the hot sun. The traveler approached one of the workers and asked him what he was doing. The man, all caked with a mixture of dirt and sweat, turned toward the traveler and, with an irritated scowl, said, "Can't you see? I'm laying stone!"

The traveler quickly backed away, excusing himself. Still curious, however, he approached another of the men laboring in the heat of the day. "Excuse me. Can you tell me what you're doing here?" This second man, bending into his work and barely turning his head toward the traveler, grunted, "Can't you see? I'm building a wall!" And then he, too, ignored the nosy visitor.

But our traveler was still curious. In his last attempt to find out the purpose of the men's work, he approached a third man. He asked again, "My good fellow, can you tell me what you're doing here in this field?" The man turned to face the traveler. He, too, was struggling with the heavy stone in the sweltering heat. He was covered from head to foot with the fine dust that hung heavy in the air. His face was streaked with sweat, but as he turned, the traveler could see a fire in his eyes, a spark of energy that was absent in the eyes of the other two men. "I'm building a great cathedral," the third man said. "A monument to God!"

Now it was clear that this third man would never live to see the inside of his great cathedral. He would never hear the sacred music rise and echo off its fan-vaulted ceilings. He would never view the brilliant glow of sunlight filtering through stained glass high above the altar. In fact, it's likely that even this man's great-great-grandson—also destined to be a stonemason—wouldn't live to see the cathedral completed. And yet, this stonemason's vision of his great monument to God gave his work meaning. It elevated his effort. It transformed his difficult work into something greater than him.

All of these men had the technical skills. Only one man had the positive attitude and passion. We can only guess how much more he put into his work!

When you lead with GRIT®, you don't hope you have positive people on board. You make sure you do. Your influence, your ripple, will inspire others to get on board.

Of course, that doesn't guarantee that everyone will get on board, and those who choose not to might need help finding a better fit elsewhere. Perhaps it's within the company but in a different department or role, or it may not be within the company at all. Keeping GRIT® in mind, we can help them find a better fit—it doesn't have to be a bitter affair.

Be mindful that as your awareness heightens, you will naturally see more, and it can be easier to pick out all the negativity. We need to be careful not to judge and criticize. Just because we can see it doesn't mean lecturing about it will be helpful. Clearly, it's not about ignoring it. Because you know how to have these conversations now, this will become much easier. (Review Chapter 9 if you need a refresher.)

Invest in People

The only thing worse than training employees and losing them is to not train them and keep them.

—Zig Ziglar

If you want GRIT® to ripple more quickly, then provide training to employees. If workers are being schooled in the concepts around GRIT®, they will embrace change and take ownership of their own experience at work. The benefits of increased productivity; less stress, burnout, and illness; and more creativity and passion will happen sooner for you, too!

To get the best return on any training investment, begin by identifying which skills are needed and who in the organization currently possesses those skills. There will be gaps. People will need to develop, and everyone has different strengths and limitations. Throughout your training endeavors, make sure you leverage the talents of each individual to support and enhance the team.

Take the lead; show that you are serious about training and open to developing yourself. Start with a 360 feedback assessment to gain other people's perceptions of your gaps. This will not only help you further develop, and maybe even find some blind spots that you weren't aware of, but also show you're not afraid to be vulnerable and take the steps necessary to improve your leadership skills.

Like anything in life, it's important to use the proper tool. 360 feedback can be a disaster if not rolled out properly, including creating a safe environment and using the right tool. My favorite is the Everything DiSC® 363 for Leaders assessment. It is simple and powerful. It integrates DiSC®, plus provides three strategies for improving your leadership effectiveness. The result is a 360 experience that's more productive and satisfying.

You'll want a cohesive program throughout your organization that has common language and themes for people to embrace. Practice, application, and tools to draw from are essential, as well as a plan to keep it alive. The most effective programs integrate into onboarding or employee orientation, executive leadership development, supervisory and other mid-level management programs, team retreats, sales, and customer loyalty programs. Working with a professional trainer and coach can make the difference in the quality and efficiency of your training programs. Treat it seriously, and you'll get a serious return on your investment.

Preventing a Tidal Wave

You can't change what you refuse to confront.

—Gina Senarighi

If you look at any number of the best practices that we've discussed, you'll see that failing to do them will get in the way of your ripple. Worth mentioning again are those internal fears and insecurities that limit many of us. Fear is often masked as negative attitudes, arrogance, blaming, taking on too much work, complaining, and a myriad of other facades. Fear gets in the way of handling issues that create the huge splashes that could wipe out our ripple.

We learned that fear tactics are commonly used as a device to control—a means of limiting questions and keeping people in check. We know that fear-based systems and philosophies end up being counterproductive, as they do little to engender loyalty or job satisfaction. When people work for the joy of it—because they love what they do and not because they've been threatened to perform—they tend to invest more of themselves in what they produce. Without fear of being judged or punished, they can more easily tap into their creativity. Many companies have begun to realize this and have transformed their culture in an effort to retain employees and improve productivity. But as we know, many more continue to rely on fear-based mechanisms for results.

As leaders, we've got to have the courage to take care of things that will get in the way of our ripple. A great example of this happened with a small professional services firm I'd been working with for a couple of years. As they struggled with getting people aligned and working toward the same goal, they realized one executive on the team was headed in a different direction. People were confused, and it was getting in the way of reaching their goals. Through an offsite retreat, together we brought this to light, and the executive became aware that it was time to part ways. He made the choice, once he could see that it didn't make sense to stay. The CEO made the right decision to create this opportunity. Since then, the firm has grown, and people are happier and more productive.

As insignificant as they may seem, when we don't handle office pet peeves, they grow into bigger issues, causing lack of engagement and, yes, tidal waves that get in the way of our ripple.

In 2011, NBC News reported the top five pet peeves in the U.S. workplace (Kennemer, 2011), according to a LinkedIn survey of about 2,000 people, with the number one being "people who don't take ownership of their actions." You know, the person who blames everything on something or someone else. They don't see, or they don't want to see, that they are responsible or at least play a part.

The second pet peeve was the constant complainers, the negative Nellies. Rather than focusing on what went right or the positive side of things, they continuously dwell on the negative and complain about things.

The third pet peeve was "people who don't clean up after themselves when using the fridge, microwave, coffee maker or other common areas." Again, such people aren't taking owner-ship of their actions.

"Boring meetings that start late or go way too long" was the fourth pet peeve. When the meeting is worse than watching paint dry, it's not structured and organized with an agenda and time line, people waltz in whenever they feel like it and the facilitator goes as long as she wants—it shows little respect for the team.

The fifth pet peeve was "people who consistently seem to miss your email." Really, it just gets blended in with all the others or lost in spam every time? When it happens once or twice, okay. When it becomes a pattern, it needs to be addressed.

What do these pet peeves have in common? You got it: There's a lack of GRIT®.

GRIT® gives us a road map to being more positive while being more creative and productive at work, at home, and in all areas of our lives. People derive more happiness from their personal lives as a result of embracing GRIT®, which leads to a more productive and satisfying work life. It's not rocket science—when you are happier, it has a ripple effect. It spreads to other areas of your life. It spreads to other people.

When you lead with GRIT®, you awaken people to their true potential, igniting passion and perseverance that get lasting results.

Before you venture into Chapter 11, take some time to reflect.

What SHIFT Will You Make?

Scan the chapter. List the topics that resonated with you.

_____

_____

Hone in on one or two areas that will make the biggest impact for you.

_____

_____

Imagine the impact. Why is this important? How will you feel when you've accomplished this?

_____

_____

Figure out your plan and how you will stay on track.

_____

_____

Take action. Start now. Schedule it now, and include your follow-up.

_____

_____

Enjoy! Remember to choose to be happy, every step of the way!

Reference

Kennemer, K. (2011). Top 5 Pet Peeves in the Workplace. Retrieved from http://thepeoplegroup.com/2011/09/top-5-pet-peeves-in-the-workplace/.

CHAPTER ELEVEN

KEEPING ON TRACK

Success is not final, failure is not fatal: it is the courage to continue that counts.

—Winston Churchill

John said he felt like a broken record. He couldn't count how many times he felt he had set clear goals, given direction, and had everyone agree on the tasks and on who was responsible, only to find that projects had slipped through the cracks, resulting in nothing even close to the expectations originally set. As a desperate measure, I got the phone call that John needed help.

We met early one Monday morning at a local coffee shop, so he could keep this meeting confidential from the rest of the company. The last thing he needed was people distracted and buzzing about this. As he shared the details of countless situations that all sounded exactly as he had first described on the phone, I could tell he was frustrated and feeling defeated. I couldn't help but wonder what domino effect this might be having on the team.

When John had vented all he needed, I replied, "It's got to be frustrating when you put all that effort into it and it doesn't work. Let's probe just a little more and see if we can find some areas that perhaps were missed. Would you be willing to do that with me?"

John was more than willing—I think he would have supported that coffee shop all day if I would have stayed with him. But we didn't need all day to figure out what was missing. John had done a great job of creating a vision and goals that people were excited about. He did the right thing by getting them all together to figure out their strategies and steps to take to get there. He started strong with getting people engaged.

What John didn't think about was what the road would be like on the way to the goal. He was focused only on the goal and getting things started. He left people to figure out their own paths without a map to guide them. Creating the initial buy-in and setting their tasks and responsibilities was a really good start, but people need continuous engagement and interaction. Like growing a garden, we can't rely only on good soil, tilling the ground, planting the seeds, and thinking only about reaping a healthy harvest. We've got to stay close, making sure there's the proper amount of water, picking the weeds, pruning the offshoots, and gathering the ripe vegetables. People need continuous connection, and systems to help them stay on track.

Transforming your workplace culture begins by envisioning a new one—one in which people can't wait to come to work.

They are open, friendly, communicating clearly and directly, and helping each other stay on track. We have to be able to see it and believe it, even before it's true. In Chapter 10, we spent time discovering what we need to do as a leader to create the ripple effect. If we spend quality time getting people on board and buying in, keeping people on track becomes much easier.

Does there need to be a system to hold people accountable? Let's stop right here for a moment and think about how that sounds. We've talked about words and how they can be negatively charged. I don't know too many people who like to be held accountable. Yes, it is what we are doing, but the intent behind it can be misunderstood when we use those words. When you're holding someone accountable, it feels like you're forcing them or catching them doing something wrong. When you're helping someone stay on track, it feels like you're in their corner. You want them to succeed. Remember, our words and our intent are powerful. Maybe some people don't mind being held accountable. Everyone is different, but I can tell you from my experience that most people don't appreciate the terminology. We can avoid a lot of wasted time and stress if we stay aware and respect the message as someone else might be hearing it.

So do we need to have systems to help people stay on track? Of course we do. As anyone who has successfully dieted can attest, the most difficult thing about change is sticking to it, especially when dealing with uncontrollable external factors. People are going to get off track. How do we know when we're off track? It takes awareness, either our own or someone or something else helping us to see it. Yes, that's why we spent so much time on awareness in Part I! When we have a way to stay on track, we are more likely to sustain the change. We spend all that time creating visions and values, getting people to understand where we are going, and training people, and we need a way to keep it alive! We're creatures of habit, and it's easy to fall back on old habits. We just need a little help—some reminders and systems to help us stay the course.

It is true you will need fewer systems because GRIT® inspires people to step up, not for the sake of reward, but out of authentic generosity—a true passion for what they do. When our purpose is strong, it is easier, but systems can support us, help us keep on track, and make it much easier to get back on track. They are great reminders, helping us to be aware and more efficient with our tasks.

Keep in mind, though, you can have the best systems, but without people's buy-in, it won't matter.

Leaders Set the Direction

The first responsibility of a leader is to define reality. The last is to say thank you. In between, the leader is a servant.
—Max De Pree

To keep on track means we as leaders have to be on track first, and that's what we were focusing on in Parts I and II. We've got to walk the talk first. Be clear and consistent with our values, who we are, and what we stand for. This is crucial for people to trust and follow us.

You've got to know where you want to go, what you want to accomplish, and who you need to help get you there. What skills, beliefs, or thoughts need to be changed to arrive at the goal? This takes understanding your team and their assets. You will need to analyze your strengths and your limitations.

People in your organization have to become a priority. In the same way we maintain our car, we need regular checkups to make sure our team is healthy and happy. Of course, we need to take it beyond how we maintain a car. In Chapter 10, we learned how to create connection. Connecting with others, on a human level, is what can make the biggest difference.

People need to know where they are going and align around the goal or the vision. Spend ample time communicating with your team. The amount of time is not a clear-cut formula. If you are connected with your team, you'll know the amount of time that's right. A friendly hint: It's usually more time than you are currently allowing.

If we really want our people to step up and take ownership, we have to empower them. So often I see managers give people responsibility but not the authority to go along with it. Managers say things like "The customer is always right, and you need to be treating them that way," but they give no authority to make decisions to support this. And then they swoop in and take over. How can our people take ownership this way? Are we really showing that we trust and believe in them?

With the right tools, technology, and systems in place to help our team achieve the goal, we show we're serious about this and we care! High-quality tools and systems are essential. If you've had the experience of poor systems or technology, you know it can wear on people and be extremely irritating. It's just plain inefficient. I consider myself a fairly positive person, and I'm even irritated at times by simple things like where they place the toilet paper roll in a hotel room bathroom and how difficult it can be to navigate a website.

If we think of ourselves as serving our people, instead of them serving us, we'll make sure we have the best tools and user friendly systems, including high-quality technology, to support their success. Serving our people might be a concept that's a bit of a stretch for some, so let's dig deeper to understand it. Servant leadership dates back to a Chinese philosopher, Lao Tzu, in 530 BCE: "The highest type of ruler is one of whose existence the people are barely aware.... The Sage is self-effacing and scanty of words. When his task is accomplished and things have been completed, all the people say, 'We ourselves have achieved it!'"

Modern-day servant leadership began when Robert Greenleaf wrote a paper, "The Servant as Leader," in 1970, stating: "The servant leader is servant first.... It begins with the natural feeling that one wants to serve, to serve first. Then conscious choice brings one to aspire to lead...(vs. one who is leader first...)." Ken Blanchard, Max De Pree, and many others have used the term *servant leadership* to help leaders embrace the concept of giving or, in the GRIT® model, generosity. In Adam Grant's recent book *Give and Take (2014)*, he notes that research supports that servant leadership creates higher productivity.

I saw servant leadership in action one day while visiting a mid-size professional service business that had been a client for about six months. The CEO was cleaning up the break room. I was surprised because you rarely see that. No one thought anything of it. When I discreetly asked one of the team members I was coaching that day, she said with a chuckle, "Oh, yeah, I guess he does do that. He seems to always clear things for us, not just the dishes!"

Rather than needing to be in the limelight, leaders like this are supporting the front line. They have the mentality of serving their people. They think about what they can do to make their people successful, not how they can catch them doing something wrong. They clear roadblocks, not create them. They make themselves available, not scarce. They offer questions and a listening ear rather than giving all the answers and telling them what to do. They build employees' confidence rather than tear it down. They remove fears rather than produce them. People feel like they're being supported, instead of feeling like they're getting thrown under the bus. Serving people is about creating the culture and putting the systems in place to support people's success.

Know the Where and the Why

Vision without action is a daydream. Action without vision is a nightmare.

—Japanese Proverb

> There's an old story about a hunter who is walking
> through the woods. He comes across hundreds of
> large colorful targets painted on all kinds of trees and
> is amazed to see that all of the arrows on all of the
> targets have hit the bull's-eyes! Never a miss! The
> hunter wanders near and far, anxious to meet this
> perfect marksman. Finally he finds him and asks,
> "Please tell me, what is the secret behind your perfect
> aim? You never miss!" The archer smiles and replies,
> "It is really quite simple. First I shoot my arrows.
> Then I paint the targets."

If we don't have direction and purpose, people will be painting their own targets.

As leaders, we should have an idea of where we want to go. You don't need to have all the details worked out, but you need to have that vision a team can strive toward. The goal should be something that is exciting and motivating to them, something inspiring that will create more energy toward achieving it. It should be something that isn't real yet—it is in the future, something they can strive toward. And the more we can help them visualize the goal, the easier it is for them to retain it, believe in it, and make it happen! Meaningful vision statements are important to aligning the team.

While it's important to be bold, vision statements need to be realistic. They can't be so pie in the sky that people won't believe it's possible. When introducing the idea to your team, let them consider it, think about it, wordsmith it a bit. Invite them to poke holes. You want them to be on board, so they need a chance to test it. This is a great opportunity for you to provide the clarity they need to understand it. You might end up changing a word or two or maybe even something more. Be open to these possibilities. Respect that there could be something you didn't consider or something that is actually just as good, if not better, that your team may help you to see.

People need an environment where they feel safe to be candid about the vision and the obstacles. If we don't address the elephants in the room, they won't go away; in fact, they grow bigger. It's best to consider everything that could be an obstacle and deal with it. Not identifying it doesn't mean it will not be there. Remember LAF with your team: Listen to what everyone has to say. Acknowledge that you heard them. Follow through on any necessary items. If there won't be a change, be up-front and let them know you appreciate the idea, thought, or suggestion. You feel strongly that it needs to be the way you have set it up. Be confident, yet humble. Make sure they feel heard.

Whenever we have people working together on a team, there will be disagreement, so make sure you clarify any issues—in a way that doesn't feel forceful, of course. Before we can move forward, we must get everyone's commitment to the goal. Even if they didn't initially agree, the leader has to ask for everyone's buy-in. Everyone must be moving in the same direction toward the goal, not painting their own targets. Otherwise, it's very difficult to ensure accountability, not just for the leader, but for teammates to help keep each other on track. Peer accountability typically has more impact than boss-employee accountability, as seen on professional sports teams and within military units.

If we create a GRIT® culture, we, too, will have the benefit of peer accountability. *Accountabili-buddies*, a term one of my class participants gave me, not only help each other stay on track but also watch each other's back. Remember the Accountability Ladder from Chapter 3 (see Figure 11.1)? When one of the team is on the bottom rungs, the rest of the team will help her see that she's there and lend

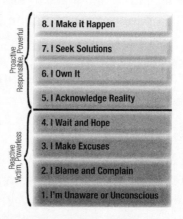

Figure 11.1. The Accountability Ladder

her a helping hand to climb to the upper rung to make things happen.

As the leader, you're the driver. You are the one with ultimate responsibility to keep yourself and the team on track. The leader is the one with a foot on the gas pedal setting a pace that keeps people moving. We don't want the engine to stall; we want it to run smoothly and efficiently. While we want people acting with a sense of urgency, we don't want recklessness that impedes our progress.

To keep on track, we've got to be looking ahead and considering what might trip us up. Are there any speed bumps that we need to slow down for or caution lights or warning signs? Looking ahead is critical to staying on track, and that means scheduling time to plan, analyze, and debrief.

Use Meetings to Keep on Track

Sometimes I get the feeling that the two biggest problems in America today are making ends meet and making meetings end.

—Robert Orben

When you hear the word *meetings*, what pops into your mind? Most of us who have experienced too many unproductive meetings will say, "Waste of time!" Too often meetings are inefficient, unproductive, and unorganized.

Meetings help people stay on track. Meetings are necessary before projects, and at the end of projects. They're where we share the vision, roll out the plans, clarify expectations and desired results, and make sure we're all on track. In meetings is where we also learn from the past by discovering what went wrong, what went right, and what we will do differently next time.

One-on-one meetings, when conducted effectively, have been known to increase productivity by as much as 50 percent. Having regular meeting times is good practice, so make sure cancellations and rescheduling don't become a pattern. Postponements erode trust, and the message most people get is that it's just not that important. Implement GRIT® into your meetings, and like your culture, you'll notice more efficiency and effectiveness immediately:

Truth: Know the purpose of the meeting. Is a meeting really necessary? What needs to be covered in the meeting? Have an agenda. Make sure you have invited all the right people, and prioritize the items in order of importance.

Integrity: Make sure the right people are included in any pre-meeting agenda items as well as in the meeting itself. Don't invite people who aren't needed. If you are unsure, give them the option to decide if they need to be there. Stick to the agenda. Use a parking lot for things outside the agenda. Follow through on items from the previous meeting. Make action items. Tackle the most important items first. Start and end on time.

Respect: Have everyone turn off gadgets, so they can be present. Give everyone an opportunity to weigh in; it's important that people are acknowledged. Respect all opinions and views. Consider the time that's really needed. Most meetings are scheduled for an hour even when less time is actually needed. For some reason, we think we need to fill up the space when we should be mindful of people's time. Stick to the schedule, arrive on time, and stay focused on the objective for the meeting. Keep things flowing, and keep it on time.

Generosity: Think of everything people need to have at the meeting to be successful. Give them all the information promptly. Make it fun while you're keeping things on track. Impose a disruption fee for anyone who is late, takes calls, texts, or is otherwise distracted.

Creating a Culture of Feedback and Recognition

There is more hunger for love and appreciation in this world than for bread.

—Mother Teresa

Feedback and recognition are critical to helping people stay on track. Then why is it that we avoid saying something that could potentially help someone and improve a situation? When you think of feedback as helping, maybe you'll be more eager to give it.

There are many formal opportunities to give feedback, such as at the end of a project and in annual performance appraisals. Particularly for managers, giving feedback could be the most impactful action you can take to make the biggest difference in your teams. Don't wait for formal opportunities. Giving feedback informally on a regular basis makes improvements happen faster and more quickly decreases your stress and workload.

Feedback, put simply, is a way to share information to reinforce what a person is doing or offer suggestions about something that needs to change. Because it's difficult to be objective about your own performance, it's necessary to have others tell us what they are seeing. Whether to keep them on track, inspire them, or help them see something that needs to change, appropriate feedback could be a person's only opportunity to be made aware. In that sense, you can see that giving feedback is a gift.

If it's given with the intention of a gift to help someone, then the way feedback comes across will be better received than if it is given harshly out of frustration or hidden behind sarcasm because we don't know how to be direct. Unfortunately, most of us avoid giving enough feedback and recognition, and across all industries and no matter the company size, I hear the same reasons.

Let's start with looking at recognition, what the training industry refers to as positive feedback.

From my experience, the top reasons managers and supervisors avoid giving positive feedback:

- It's their job. Why should I have to tell them what they're doing right?
- It sounds cliché.
- They'll expect a raise if I tell them too many good things.
- I don't need to hear positive feedback. Why should they?

A recent Harris poll (Colan, 2012) found that around 65 percent of workers were receiving no recognition for good work. Consider what positive recognition does. Think back to a time someone genuinely and specifically told you about something you did that really helped the team or the company or a customer. Were you more motivated to keep working hard or less motivated? Exactly! When we give sincere, specific feedback to help someone see what they're doing right and that we appreciate it, it inspires them to want to do more. Giving recognition for the things that people are doing right is about showing your appreciation, your gratitude.

Giving positive feedback is easy with GRIT®, using generosity, respect, integrity, and truth. We always start with truth, which leads to generosity:

Truth—Be mindful of what people are doing; look for the positive things.

Integrity—Be specific. Include the details of what they did that is right. Be timely; let them know when you see it.

Respect—Let them know the value of what they did and how it affected the team or the customer or the company. Be mindful of DiSC® styles. Be aware that some people don't like public recognition. Only give it in public if there is a higher benefit and it won't embarrass the person. Some people aren't comfortable with it at all. You may need to coach them on receiving recognition.

Generosity—Give plenty of it. Not too much so it becomes meaningless, but enough so it helps a person stay on track. Positive recognition can help build a person's confidence, as well as increase his level of trust and respect for you.

An obvious and easy example of positive recognition is to just say thank you. "John, I really appreciate the way you quickly and diplomatically resolved that customer's issue. I noticed you were careful to not add costs for us, too. That makes a huge difference to the company. Thank you."

Keep in mind that motivation for true engagement needs to be intrinsic. Obviously, employees need a fair and adequate compensation plan in place, but with money taken out of the picture, motivation lies within intrinsic areas. People want to feel they have control of their lives and are not being micromanaged. This shows you trust them. People also want to grow and develop. Remember, our brains crave it, and people want to be a part of a bigger picture, like the stonemason. They want to feel that what they are doing has meaning and purpose.

Companies that focus on these areas for motivation will see employee satisfaction, retention, innovation, and productivity rise. So when you're giving positive recognition, remember to tie it into the intrinsic factors.

Constructive feedback is also essential for keeping people on track, but it is often avoided. The top reasons that managers and supervisors avoid giving constructive feedback:

- I don't know how to say it in a way that will come across helpful.
- I feel uncomfortable—don't like confrontation.
- I hope it will take care of itself.
- I don't have time to deal with it.

If we keep it in mind that we are helping someone, we'll be more eager to give feedback and the way we say it will improve. Just think about how you say something when you're helping someone versus how you say something when you're angry, frustrated, jealous, upset—your tone of voice, pitch, volume, and words are completely different. Remember that 93 percent of a message someone receives is from nonverbal communication. Even when you strive to find the right words, your frustration and anger are coming through loud and clear. By the way, this typically happens because we've waited way too long to say something.

Give constructive feedback with GRIT®: generosity, respect, integrity, and truth. Again, we start with truth, which leads to generosity:

Truth—Be mindful of what the truth is and what it is not. Understand the facts of the situation, and don't assume secondhand information is true. Strive to find the truth of the situation first.

Integrity—Say it directly and to the point, and keep it focused on the issue, not the person. Choose your battles; not every issue needs attention.

Respect—Say it with a helpful intent and with consideration of the person's DiSC® style. Keep it private. Realize that you may not have the whole truth. Ask questions if you need to. Let them know the impact, what it is causing. Pause and give the person an opportunity to share information.

Generosity—Help the person with a solution or training, or give encouragement that they can make a change.

Let's look at an example of a person who reacts to positive feedback by expecting a raise: She most likely did it jokingly, but we all know there's truth behind the kidding. Address it. Your feedback might go something like this (with a helpful intent):

> It's true Mary; you did a great job on the fountain project. It's exactly what I expected you to do. I know you jokingly said, "Where's my raise?" I just want you to know I need to be recognizing you more for the things you're doing right. Even though it's part of your job, I really do appreciate when you do it well. [pause] If there's anything I can do to help you, you let me know.

Leading with GRIT® sets the stage for giving and receiving feedback. When you get a negative reaction to the feedback, respect where that person might be, and don't let it throw you off track. Remain on course with the message, while staying open and being helpful.

Sharing information with people to help them stay on track is not only a gift but also our responsibility as leaders. Remember the law of giving and receiving: Give people the gift of feedback, and you'll receive many benefits, in ways you won't even expect.

Once we believe in giving feedback, we may need to create systems to remind us to actually do it. I remember using rubber bands on my arm to remind me to give positive feedback. I was a new supervisor, and I just wasn't in the habit of doing it. I believed in giving positive feedback, but I was racing around trying to get all those other tasks completed and neglecting to do it. Use whatever system works for you, but set up reminders to keep yourself on track.

You Need Feedback Too

Feedback is the breakfast of champions.

—Ken Blanchard

With all this attention given to delivering effective feedback, we often overlook the benefits of soliciting it. Feedback provides an opportunity to validate and measure our effectiveness. Without it, leaders are forced to rely on their own self-perception, and we know what that can look like: FIGJAM, an Australian acronym shared by a class participant meaning "Frig I'm Good, Just Ask Me!"

There's enormous value to be found in getting feedback from employees. Employees reveal information about their personal stressors and motivators, which will help us serve more effectively. By listening, acknowledging, and following through (LAF), leaders build loyalty and trust. And, hey, isn't it great you can continue to LAF with your team!

Congruency is the key. Saying that feedback is welcomed and encouraged needs to be backed up with actions. Some employees refrain from giving feedback to their manager—especially constructive feedback—because they fear retaliation. Others feel that feedback is the privilege of people with titles. As leaders, we must be open to receive feedback if we truly want to stay on course.

The following are tips to keep in mind for soliciting feedback:

- Don't assume that silence means everything is fine. Pay attention to employees' behaviors. Do you see facial expressions that hint of disapproval? Do you hear frustration in a voice? Are they avoiding you?

- When you see these signs, first be aware of your own assumptions around the nonverbals. They are not facts; they are hints to be explored. Acknowledge them. Share your perception with employees in an asking tone to get clarification. This will open the door and invite feedback.

- Ask, don't guess. Build in routine checkpoints. Ask employees for input. Ask them how they feel about a project. Ask them how you might be more supportive of them.

- Don't take it personally or react defensively; receive feedback gracefully. Thank them. Once you've opened the door, nothing will close it faster than a defensive reaction. Remember, you don't have to agree with their perception. Simply listening, acknowledging, and communicating is often enough to build trust and open lines of communication.

Remember John, the broken record? Two years after we completed our work together, we met for coffee. He was happy to report he was finally staying on track. He kept close to his people, gave them the tools and encouragement they needed, helped them stay on track all along the way, and guess what? John's record hasn't skipped once since then!

Complaints Aren't Always Bad

When complaints are freely heard, deeply considered and speedily reformed, then is the utmost bound of civil liberty attained that wise men look for.

—John Milton

I've learned a lot in life about what not to do, which has helped me stay on track. I've had bosses and peers I've watched and I've decided I would never do what they did. Admittedly, I've made my own mistakes that taught me valuable lessons as well. So let's take a look at the top complaints that employees have about upper management and the leadership team. In my experience, these are common across all industries and geographical boundaries, but don't take my word for it: Ask your employees. It's a great opportunity to practice soliciting feedback.

The number one complaint I hear is about control freaks, you know, those bosses who just can't let go. They are constantly checking up on you, looking over your shoulder, fixing every single thing you did to make what you are working on absolutely picture perfect. It's annoying, demeaning, and frustrating. These micromanagers are obsessed with controlling projects and people. They don't trust that anyone can do it as well as they can. What they don't realize is that they are disempowering their employees and causing work performance to decrease. In some cases, they are actually deteriorating employees' confidence. Often what results is that top employees leave and go to work elsewhere.

How do I remedy this, you ask? Know your employees, in particular, their DiSC® styles, their preferences, and their passions, which will help you understand how much autonomy they prefer. Set clear expectations and deadlines, and provide any training they need.

People expect that they will receive clear expectations and training, and when they don't, they may not feel comfortable asking for it. Managers need to create an environment where people feel safe to ask and even invite it.

Remain open and available for them to contact you with questions. Then give them the freedom to do the job you have empowered them to do. Agree on how you'll check in. It's good practice to check in periodically just to say, "Hey, how's it going?" but refrain from taking over. If you notice they are off track, you can gently guide them back by asking questions and asking permission to show them.

At the top of the list of complaints is that upper management is unapproachable or not accessible. Leaders are busy people, no doubt, but their tendency to isolate themselves from employees ironically will make them even busier in the long run. Their offices are far away, and you rarely see them on the floor. When you do, the energy changes, and everyone acts uptight. They give off an air of being so busy and important that people avoid them.

We've covered a lot on this remedy in Part II and in Chapter 10. Another good idea is to walk around regularly. Pop in and out of different departments to say hello and find out what is going on. Show people you care. Do your best to remember names, interests people have, and family. LAF (listen, acknowledge, and follow through) with people, and laugh with people—it's good for the soul and good for the relationship. Create venues for conversation: town hall meetings, lunches, happy hours. Set some guidelines to help people talk to you openly and candidly. Remember to thank people for suggestions and feedback. Don't make excuses. Be direct and honest, but not negative. Most people just want to be heard and acknowledged and to feel that you care.

Right up there with the other two complaints is lack of feedback. In most organizations, people complain that there simply isn't any feedback of any kind. No one is saying anything. When they do, it's usually negative, both in content and in delivery. Managers wait until they are so fed up that they end up saying things that just aren't helpful and most likely will not improve the situation. If it does, there may be other repercussions related to the poor delivery of feedback that will be hard to recognize.

Rarely if ever is there positive recognition. When there is, it's usually vague, like "Great job, Joe." There's not a lot put into it. Most managers are saving up all their feedback for performance appraisal time. Think of all the wasted opportunity if you don't continuously check in and provide guidance. It'd be like trying to maintain your car without changing the oil and then wondering why you have a lot of other very costly things going wrong with it.

A rule of thumb is to average about three times as much positive recognition as constructive feedback. Make it sincere and specific. This builds trust, and it's easier to talk about the things that need to change if you've built up someone's confidence. That's obviously an average. It will depend on your culture and the individual. Whatever your ratio, it's important to provide recognition to help people stay on track.

Complaints can be useful, and we can learn a lot from them. So don't avoid them; be open to them. Solicit feedback and listen.

Get Them Off the Tracks!

Employees with toxic behavior can derail and jeopardize your path to success. Take ownership and reshuffle the deck. It will be painful in the short term, but preventative action is your leverageable asset.

—Cindy Wahler

I once had an employee who on paper looked great. I didn't do the proper interview, and, well, you can see where this is going. She didn't fit what I needed, and she wasn't happy doing the work she was hired to do. I needed to let her go, and yes, I waited way too long. It was grueling. I wasn't fully aware of GRIT® then, and I was sick over the situation. Remember that our emotions are triggers. For me, this was an opportunity to be aware. Although I knew intellectually that this was the right thing to do, it wasn't making me feel any better. GRIT® gives us the courage and certainty to do the right thing. It helps us use our intuition more than our heads.

Even when we do a proper interview, sometimes, no matter how well we set it all up, there will be some people who are not on board. Keeping that toxic person, usually because they have some necessary technical skill, can be a costly mistake. Most of us have experienced this situation, and when the person is finally released, there is a sigh of relief and an increase in motivation and productivity. Keeping on track also means removing those who are getting other people off track.

Think about it logically for a moment. Why hold someone somewhere they don't fit? Would you keep a puzzle piece that doesn't belong just because it almost fits? Even in a personal relationship, you can see that this doesn't make any sense. Give the person freedom. Realize that you may have to help the person make that choice. With GRIT®, this process is with truth, integrity, respect, and, yes, generosity.

Your team may question your judgment if you don't take action to remove someone from the team. I've heard countless complaints from team members on this very topic. Ironically, many leaders don't realize this, most likely because they're too close to the emotional aspect of it. People respect the leader who makes the tough calls because they trust that person is looking out for the team.

I know, being a leader can feel like drinking from a fire hose—there's so much coming at you, it can feel completely overwhelming. That's why GRIT® is so helpful: to align us to the most important things, so we can handle what it takes to lead and enjoy the journey.

Before you venture into Chapter 12, take some time to reflect.

What SHIFT Will You Make?

Scan the chapter. List the topics that resonated with you.

_____

_____

Hone in on one or two areas that will make the biggest impact for you.

_____

_____

Imagine the impact. Why is this important? How will you feel when you've accomplished this?

_____

_____

Figure out your plan and how you will stay on track.

_____

_____

Take action. Start now. Schedule it now, and include your follow-up.

_____

_____

Enjoy! Remember to choose to be happy, every step of the way!

_____

_____

References

Colan, L. (2012). Employee Appreciation: Take it personally. Retrieved from http://www.thelgroup.com/p_theletter/257.asp.

Grant, A. (2014). *Give and Take: Why helping others drives our success.* New York, New York: Penguin Books.

Greenleaf, Robert. (1970). The Servant as Leader. Westfield, Indiana: Robert K. Greenleaf Center.

CHAPTER TWELVE

ENJOY THE JOURNEY

If people believe in themselves, it's amazing what they can accomplish.

—Sam Walton

When we fully embrace GRIT®, we become authentic and free—not so easily affected by others' negativity. We accept the reality of life, and we look at it more positively. We believe in ourselves, and we believe that life is something we have a right to enjoy. We're not supposed to be suffering. We realize that we are responsible for what we've created, or at least we play a part in it. We can choose at any moment to be positive and happy. At home, at work, in our social lives—we can enjoy it all. It doesn't mean that stuff doesn't happen. But we know we can make the best choices for ourselves, and when stuff does happen, we deal with it. We choose to continue to be happy while dealing with it.

We accept where we are today, while striving to grow and continuously improve. We are able to look at ourselves and others with new eyes every day because we respect that we are all changing and growing. To improve doesn't mean anything was wrong with us to begin with. Sometimes people think if they are look-ing to change or improve, it must be because they aren't okay the way they are. For example I've met with executives who initially resisted training because they didn't want the team to get the mes-sage that they are broken and need fixing.

If we look at the happiest, most successful people and com-panies, they're those that have a positive attitude about continu-ously improving. It's growth. It's something new. It's an adventure. We realize that to change doesn't mean we're rejecting who we are. We relish the opportunities we have to explore life, to try new things. We don't need something in the future to look forward to; rather, we balance being happy with where we are right now and looking forward to the future. And we're not afraid of what the future holds. We trust that everything really will be okay—better than okay. It will be rocking, awesome, fantabulous, and cool! Let's explore a few ways to help us enjoy the journey.

No Need to Worry

Don't Worry; Be Happy.

—Meher Baba

When we don't worry, we are able to let go of the little things that bother us without ignoring patterns and trends that may need to be addressed. We know the things that are really important to us, and we make choices that align. We make time for self-reflection, to be still in the moment, to recharge our batteries. With an objective view, it's so much easier to identify the things that we can let go of and stop letting them eat away at us. We know what we can and cannot control, and we don't try to change the things we can't control. Instead, we look at things objectively and decide where to focus our attention.

Worrying is just thinking the worst, and it is a big waste of time. When we worry we are afraid that something bad is going to happen. We dwell on it, and there's really nothing we can do about it. Fear creeps in, and the energy around it is repelling. As mentioned, our thoughts and beliefs have a profound effect on us. If we go to bed worrying about something, we may not sleep well, and we will most likely wake up feeling tired and grumpy.

On the other hand, if we put it out there in a positive way and ask our subconscious (or God, or the universe or whomever you talk to) for help with an issue or problem, we are much more likely to get something positive as a result. Don't confuse problem solving with worry. There are things we need to figure out and solve. But worrying is worthless and creates nothing but negative energy.

For example, if you are worried about money, think about the things you say to yourself. It's usually around scarcity—there's not enough. Think about the feeling you get in your body. It's typically a tightness and closing up. Now think about when you have enough money: How do you feel? It's usually open. When we're open, rather than closed, things flow to us. If we close up, we stop the flow.

The act of worry seems to have been glorified in our culture. People have learned to believe that if you worry, it means you really care or love that person. Just like many other traits and behaviors, when they are rewarded with attention or glorification in any way, it encourages people to continue them. Suffering, worrying, being overly generous—it's romanticized, and people continue the behavior. People mistake this for connection with each other.

There's a fine line between worry, and respecting, caring, and loving someone. When we worry, we don't really believe in the person. We are afraid they have made the wrong choices or they won't be able to take care of themselves. The big bad world will just eat them up. When we care and respect someone, we put out positive thoughts and beliefs in them. We ask that good things and choices flow their way. But we don't have negative, fear-based thoughts and dwell on all the bad things that might happen.

While we don't let the little things bother us or consume our-selves with worry, we don't ignore patterns of behavior that need to be changed. There may be things that aren't working for us or for the people we care for. With GRIT®, we don't make a big deal about it. We simply align, changing our thoughts and/or behavior to better fit what we need. Or we help others to see what we're seeing and how it might help them. We don't need a lot of drama around it. It is what it is.

When we are no longer driven by fear, obsessed with what others think and feel, assuming the worst, or even performing halfheartedly, we are free to be enthusiastic and positive about our jobs and our colleagues. This can only mean good things for our organizations—and for us personally.

When we get rid of useless worrying we enjoy the journey. The rewards flow. It's the way the universe works. As we know, it attracts the right energy. You are open to receive.

Reap Your Crop

Be not deceived; God is not mocked: for whatsoever a man soweth, that shall he also reap.

—Galatians 6:7

We've heard this throughout our lives: What we sow, so shall we reap. Karma. What we put out there is what we'll get back. Most of us understand this law of nature. Just think about farmers. If they plant corn, they don't expect to get string beans. And with planting the corn, they know there are things they need to do to keep the plants healthy and alive.

If we walk around planting seeds of worry, seeds of discourage-ment, seeds of gloom and doom, seeds of despair, seeds of harm, guess what we will reap?

Perhaps emitting positive vibes just because it's a good thing to do, isn't enough to convince you. Then do it first because you know you'll get something back (it's the law of nature). Eventually you won't do it just because of what you think you'll get back—you'll do it naturally, and even more good things will flow your way.

Implementing fun at work is a way to give off positive vibes, and contrary to old beliefs, it increases creativity and productivity. The way you have fun will differ depending on your organization. A bank may need to be a little more conservative due to people's perception of handling their money, so the way they play will be different from, say, a marketing firm that gets wild with slides and romp rooms! Get people involved. Find out what they like to do for fun. If you've been practicing Part II, your asking and listening skills are primed to do this well!

At every step in our journeys, we need to celebrate and enjoy the process. When we are only waiting to achieve the goal, we can end up feeling empty and unfulfilled once we get there. The old adage "Enjoy the journey" is a great reminder.

Unsung Heroes

The time men spend in trying to impress others they could spend in doing the things by which others would be impressed.

—Frank Romer

Preventive measures don't usually create heroes because, as we covered in Chapter 10, these acts often go unnoticed. Too often we think of leadership as swooping in and saving the day. Like the unsung heroes, many actions that we take to make sure our companies are safe, enjoyable, and productive go unrecognized.

Similar to when you have an injury and it is causing you pain, you dwell on it; when something is wrong with your team, it's very noticeable. When that pain goes away, you forgot it was even there and what you had to do to heal it—and what you need to do to prevent it. When things are running smoothly in our departments, we forget the things we need to do to maintain it. What we do to stay healthy, those preventive steps we take for our health or in our companies, often go unnoticed. You are the unsung hero in your own life.

With GRIT®, we don't need to be recognized for doing the right things. We feel good ourselves and that spreads, and that's enough. Similar to schoolteachers, you may make a big impact on a person, you may prevent them from going down the wrong path, or you may steer them in a direction they never would have known. You might not ever hear back from that person about the impact you made on his life. But you know you had an impact. You trust in what you are doing and the ability and potential of people to embrace it. GRIT® creates a great balance of humility and confidence.

Once we are leading with GRIT®, although we don't need recognition, it's still a good thing to give it and gracefully accept it. So let people know the impact they made in your life. Just say thanks. Send a note. Pick up the phone and let them know they made a difference. This spreads the positive energy. Let someone know they opened a door to an opportunity for you to be happier.

With GRIT®, we don't need to be a hero. The reward of the life we now have is enough. You wake up in the morning eager to start your day, knowing you will enjoy it, and excited to make a difference in other people's lives—and your own.

Awareness gives us freedom and responsibility to make choices. Without awareness, we don't even know what choices we have, and therefore, we will not have options. Awareness alone creates a shift. You are now in the know. With awareness comes the responsibility to choose what's right for you.

As the world, our workplaces, and our roles continue to experience change, GRIT® is more important than ever. It would be easy for leaders in organizations to freeze up in facing change or try to tackle new problems with outdated means. GRIT® inspires us to take action and be accountable. It helps us stay aligned, respect change, and rather than resist it, flow with it. The principles of GRIT® are tried-and-true and will sustain us through challenging times and transform our experiences to ones we will accept and enjoy.

Remember to take some time to reflect. Build it into your life. The rewards are immeasurable.

What SHIFT Will You Make?

Scan the chapter. List the topics that resonated with you.

_____

_____

Hone in on one or two areas that will make the biggest impact for you.

_____

_____

Imagine the impact. Why is this important? How will you feel when you've accomplished this?

_____

_____

Figure out your plan and how you will stay on track.

_____

_____

Take action. Start now. Schedule it now, and include your follow-up.

_____

_____

Enjoy! Remember to choose to be happy, every step of the way!

_____

_____

● INDEX

Page references followed by *fig* indicate an illustrated figure.